Fritzi's approach to sharin
encountered as a professiona
many of the other books on ⌐. ....ay. *This powerful and*
insightful book not only chronicles her experiences of working
with the concerns and worries of adult children about ensuring
their parents' safety and security in their living environment,
while assuring they are addressed with dignity and deference, it
is also layered with practical tips and pointers embedded within
the lines of each story.

I highly recommend her book for people just beginning the
journey of ensuring quality eldercare for loved ones and for
seasoned caregivers who may be feeling a loss of energy and
strength as they continue to provide ongoing support with grace
and grit. I wish this book had been a part of my library during
my caregiving years.

— Paulette M. Bethel, PhD, CMC, President
Land On Your Feet, LLC *Anywhere in the World*™

What a lovely book! Fritzi Gros-Daillon's **Grace and Grit** *teaches*
us lessons in kindness, empathy and love. It's written with
sensitivity and humor. I will gladly recommend this book to my
clients who are preparing for their senior transitions.

— Kathleen Mazza, President, Island Transitions,
a Long Island senior move management firm

Fritzi Gros-Daillon found her voice in her new collection, **Grace**
and Grit, *where she shares her insight on aging gracefully*
in the new millennium. With so many options available to
our aging population, her personal experiences and expertise
are compassionately explored in each chapter. Her authentic
narratives touch on subjects that range from the mundane
necessities of packing to the delicate, emotional transformations
of all the individuals involved. Her sensitive portrayals create an
opportunity to have those challenging but necessary conversations
with the ones we love. I can attest to Fritz's wisdom after recently
moving my mother into a retirement community; it was a smooth
transition with the benefit of her insights.

— Jennifer Turner
San Diego, California

This book is an anthology of people's stories gathered by Fritzi to illustrate many aspects of later-life moves to assisted living. Connecting deeply with each story is easy even if neither you nor a parent is anywhere near making such a transition. No one in my direct lineage ever lived in an assisted living facility, and I myself have never needed to assist any family member in making such a transition. I have been there for others, however, and watched up close how it affects everyone on every side of the move. Clearly, Fritzi has quite a heart and comes to it with great depth of humanity.

Story after story, Fritzi touches on one aspect or another. Sometimes, the stories illustrate exceptions to the rule. It is common for family members to fight over things, but in one story, no one seems to want anything! Items the couple had hoped to pass down to their children and grandchildren are little more than trash or fodder for the donation truck to the family. A dining room set in the family for three generations just given up to be sold. Fritzi, with a great big heart, notes that these things can mean so much because we can remember our own childhood and remember raising our children with that dining room set in so many of the pictures—and the great memories are ours and ours alone. Others may not have treasured memories connected to such things.

Age comes for us all. Need comes for us all. It is simple as that. Sometimes it comes slowly, and sometimes it comes upon us suddenly. If we are prepared by the simple realization that it does happen, we can be more ready for it than we otherwise would. Certainly this book is a great help to those of us who are thinking about the future, and an equally great help for those of us coping with the recent past.

— Scot Conway, Ph.D., J.D.
8th Degree Black Belt Martial Arts Master
Author/Speaker/Trainer

Fritzi Gros-Daillon's **Grace and Grit** continually shows her love of people, concern for people and kindness for others, will help anyone in need reading her FANtabulous book.

— Judi Betts, President, Magnolia Manor Ltd.,
Port Jefferson, NY

Grace

AND *Grit*

Grace AND Grit

Insights to Real-Life Challenges of Aging for Adult Children and Their Parents

Fritzi Gros-Daillon

Pink Tulip Press
Vista, California

Publisher's Cataloging-In-Publication Data
(Prepared by The Donohue Group, Inc.)

Gros-Daillon, Fritzi.
    Grace and grit : insights to real-life challenges of aging for adult children and their parents / Fritzi Gros-Daillon.

    pages ; cm

    Issued also as an ebook.
    Includes bibliographical references and index.
    ISBN: 978-0-9914948-0-4 (paperback)

    1. Aging parents—Psychology. 2. Adult children of aging parents—Psychology. 3. Older people—Housing—Psychological aspects. 4. Moving, Household—Psychological aspects. 5. Life change events—Anecdotes. I. Title.

HQ1063.6 .G76 2014
306.874

ISBN: 978-0-9914948-0-4 (paperback)
ISBN: 978-0-9914948-1-1 (e-book)

Pink Tulip Press
993C South Santa Fe Avenue, Suite 80
Vista, California 92083
www.PinkTulipPress.com

Cover Design: Anita Jones, Another Jones Graphics
Interior Design: Julie Murkette, Satya House

Printed in the United States of America

This book is joyfully dedicated to my mom —
my first best friend

Acknowledgements

With all my heart, I would like to acknowledge all of you who have helped bring this book to the world: to my son, Vincent, my wise, loving pillar of support; to Marilou for her masterful wordsmithing to bring the stories to life; to Audra for getting our message out; to Evelyn for her keen eye; to Sharon and her team, Anita and Julie, for making the book a reality.

And to all my dear family and friends on both coasts; these stories are yours and mine—they are gifts we all share—your love and support keep me going.

CONTENTS

PROLOGUE

"I'm so worried about what to do . . . why can't there be one place I can call to get help?"

It's 2001 and I am stirring the gravy for the turkey I am about to serve to my husband John and a dozen of his closest friends. We started the tradition of the Harvest Party back in 1994, a year and some months after I married him. Long enough into knowing him to see the need to have one event each year to reunite friends, now mostly couples, who because of children, jobs and geography, found it difficult to see each other.

That first year, everyone arrived at our farm-ranch home on the North Shore of Long Island expecting something akin to a happy hour with beer, wine and appetizers. But I had a surprise for everyone, including my new husband, and welcomed them with a formal, full Thanksgiving dinner instead. So what might have been an hour or two of impersonal exchange turned into an entire evening of sit-down, getting reacquainted fellowship.

If measured in laughter and volume, the event was so successful it brought my son Vince, then nine, out of his room to check to see if everything was okay.

"It's just that they're so loud," he said as explanation for his concern.

"They'll quiet down after dinner," I promised, and kept my fingers crossed. But Big John was big in every way: six foot three inches and three hundred pounds of big heart and big laughter, big hugs and big stories. In his company, we all became "bigger" too.

By evening's end, the conversation had quieted and in the aftermath of anecdotes and tall tales, it was unanimously agreed that the get-together would be called "The Harvest Party", and that it would be held every year, two Saturdays before Thanksgiving. I kept ownership of the turkey dinner, but the others gladly took over appetizers, desserts and plenty more beer and wine.

Seven years later, we are settled into the tradition and by now the others know to leave me to tend the dinner preparation while they comfortably catch up on each other's lives in the great room. Occasionally, someone calls out my name to check on me, or check on dinner's progress. I assure them I've got it under control, and hope saying it will make it so.

Tonight I'm a bit preoccupied as I whisk the flour into the grease droppings, casually optimistic that I might just once create the right consistency for perfect gravy. I am ready to leave the environmental consulting company I've been working for the past twelve years and am thinking about what I want to do next. I am restricted by a non-compete agreement that prevents me from working for someone else in the same industry and I think that suits me; I am ready for a change and I'm thinking it may be time to start my own company, fashion my own "perfect" job, something I've wanted to do for a while. My mind is racing with possibilities and I feel the pressure of getting it "right".

On this particular evening though, as I listen to the conversations that carry from the other room, it strikes me, with something akin to divine inspiration, that there is a common, dominant theme among our friends as they share where they are in their lives: they are worried about their parents.

One friend has a recently widowed mom living thirty miles away that she gladly visits every Saturday. She buys her mother's groceries, checks on meds, and they enjoy lunch together. But because she works full-time during the week, setting aside a full day each weekend takes a toll. She is expressing to the group how much easier it would be if her mom was living in the same town as she, how much less she'd worry if she could see her mom during the week, and be closer if something unexpected happened.

Another friend chimes in that her parents are in their eighties, that her dad just had surgery and her mom is showing increasing signs of dementia, and she's not sure they can continue to live by themselves. Even though she lives only a few miles away from her parents, she still worries about them and feels the burden of their really not being able to care for themselves in a way that lets her sleep well at night.

Another couple, friends of John's since high school, bemoans the difficulty of caring for parents that live in Florida, the mother recently diagnosed as legally blind and the father growing more confused and unreliable as he attempts to shoulder the additional responsibilities for her care.

That they love their parents and feel genuine concern is clear in how they describe their predicaments and their frustration over what to do. But they are among their closest friends, allies who can feel the anguish beneath their words as they, too, struggle to make the "right" choice.

"I'm so worried about what to do," our friend says. *"Why can't there be one place I can call to get help?"*

The heartfelt conversations of that day ultimately led me to create a company called TransitionsUSA, and over the next ten years, my team would be responsible for moving over a thousand adult seniors from their homes to alternative living arrangements when circumstances required they make a change. We became a go-to resource for adult children when practical concerns prevailed and parents had to be relocated out of their homes. We sorted, down-sized, packed and moved senior adults' life possessions, aspiring to do so with compassionate regard, efficiency and kindness.

It was a role that suited me, one where everything came together to align with my highest values, values largely instilled by my mother. Nancy Turner lived a life of service to others. For her, looking out for others was done without celebration or glory or fanfare. If she could help make someone else's life easier, lighter, or—even if just in some small way—better, then she simply did so. It was the way she moved through life.

By all her words and actions, she infused that same commitment to service in my brothers and me, as children and as adults.

For me, TransitionsUSA was more than just a thing to do: facilitating the elderly has become a deep, personal calling, a way of approaching each day that carries all my commitment, compassion and vision. I have assumed a role of advocacy on behalf of aging adults that is as natural to me as breathing. I feel duty bound to educate and facilitate those who care for them—professionals and loved ones alike—and share alternatives and solutions that can make aging adults' lives richer and more independent.

I believe the world, our nation, your community, your loved ones, are facing unique challenges today when aging forces us out of our homes. These are unique challenges because the generations largely affected by this growing segment have enjoyed more freedom, more independence, and greater self-sufficiency than any generation before them. They have lived longer, carried on after the death of a spouse, perhaps even started new lives only to one day be faced with the practical reality that a failing mind or body is forcing them out of their homes, costing them what they have experienced as their freedom. In my experience, this loss of freedom can be a far greater burden than the physical loss of their homes, but loss it is. And with that loss come the Kubler-Ross five stages of grief: denial, anger, bargaining, depression, and acceptance. I believe that most of the conflict, stress and tension that show up during these transitional times emanates from the manifestation of these grieving emotions.

Remarkably though, it is not only the elderly adult who is processing grief and loss. So, too, are the children of these adults. The responsible children of the elderly adult may not be losing freedom per se, but may be struggling with their own loss of a childhood home, the loss of their perception of their parent as vital and strong, the loss of their role as protected rather than protector. Or, they could be feeling some loss of their own sense of personal freedom as they assume responsibility for a parent.

I have seen it all. I have seen every imaginable conflict, felt every tension, and witnessed every harsh word you can conjure in the course of this transition. I have also beheld, in almost tangible form, the love between parent and child: the compassion, understanding and humor that rise from the hearts of both parent and child in strained and impossible circumstances.

It may be that none of us can really predict how we'll respond to the challenges of aging until each of us is that adult child dealing with an elderly parent, or is the elderly parent faced with moving from our home. My hope is that we all may find some resonance in these vignettes about the lives of those who could be our neighbors, our own loved ones, ourselves. My hope is that by sharing some of the stories of those I've encountered along the way and the insights I've gleaned, three generations—my mother's, mine, and my son's—might collectively perpetuate just a little more "Grace and Grit".

*The problems of aging present an opportunity to rethink
our social and personal lives in order to ensure
the dignity and welfare of each individual.*
— Daisaku Ikeda

CHAPTER ONE

"Talk to me, don't talk to my daughter!"

"He's a real bastard," my friend tells me over the phone. She has her own moving service and it's a small community; we're friendly competitors and she's just come from the home of the client I'm headed toward now.

"Really? That bad?" I ask into my cell phone as I negotiate traffic. It's Christmas Eve day and the mall traffic is fierce. I've tried to go around it, but am caught up just the same.

"Well, maybe not as in a total bastard, but he's definitely not nice," she modifies.

"Any indication of whether you got the job?"

"I hope not," she says with a laugh and signs off wishing me luck.

Thirty minutes of side streets later, I arrive at the house with three minutes to spare and ring the buzzer. The door is immediately opened by the man I presume to be the prospective client, Charles. Even without a smile on his face, he looks at least ten years younger than his 88 years. He's right at six feet tall, well dressed in dark dress slacks and a pressed, button-up striped shirt. An African-American, his hair is still dark and closely trimmed, with only slight patches of gray along his temples. He waves me in with little more than a glance and turns for me to follow.

"They're still busy talking about me," he says over his shoulder with a head jerk toward the living room on the left.

"No reason we can't get on with this without her. Anyway, she'll join us soon enough." He's talking about his daughter Rose from Roanoke, Virginia, who has come for the holidays specifically to deal with moving her father to an assisted living apartment.

I glance in the room as we pass by and see yet another senior adult moving professional friend seated with a trim, attractive woman in her late fifties. I acknowledge my friend with a nod but don't wait to see if he looks up. Charles, physically spry, has already made it to the bedroom and has started pointing out what he intends to keep.

"I'm taking the bed," he states flatly and seems to plant both feet, glaring directly at me, apparently waiting to be challenged.

"Okay," I respond cautiously. In the initial phone contact, Rose had indicated Charles would be moving into a 350 square foot studio apartment. The bed is a queen, a space hog in the scheme of things.

"I've got a girlfriend so there's no arguing about it," he adds with a defiant wave of his hand.

I'm less inclined to argue than to give him a high five. But instead I play it cool and just nod in a worldly and knowing way. "What about the dresser?" I ask.

It's a nice piece of furniture, but probably sixty inches wide. Another hog.

"That goes too," he insists. "The bed and the dresser. And that little table I use for my alarm clock. And don't even think about telling me I can't take my piano."

Charles's manner is just short of belligerent, and laced with heavy doses of petulance.

"Dad, now you know we've already talked about this," Rose chides as she enters the room. She looks a lot like an amicable version of her father, the same features, and the same sharp, intelligent eyes.

"You mean, you've talked about it," he huffs and she smiles ruefully at me. We go through formal introductions and she reiterates the circumstances: her father is remarkably capable for his age, but has failing eyesight and an underlying heart condition. They no longer trust his living alone and unsupervised. She and her sister Violet in Tampa, Florida have decided to compromise space for quality and are opting for a studio apartment in a care community they trust. She is gracious but I can feel her exasperation. She doesn't look at her father as she talks; obviously, he has heard it all before.

"Outvoted and overruled," he complains under his breath. And then, in reaction to her explanation for his need for assisted care, he interrupts more loudly: "So you say, but how do you explain that I just moved myself all by myself to Florida? Didn't need anybody then to tell me what I could and could not do, take this, can't take that. Moved there myself and then turned around eight months later and did it all over again coming back. I've been taking care of myself just fine, thank you very much."

Rose interprets. "Dad is active—very active considering his age. And yes, he managed his own move to Florida and when that didn't work out quite the way we wanted, he handled coming back. He's quite mentally alert. In fact, he still teaches bridge at the community center—"

"And that's another thing. I'm going to need all my bridge stuff!"

"—but these past few months, his eyesight has gotten worse—"

"I see well enough to read my sheet music and I'm taking that piano, end of discussion!"

"—and we're just so worried that his heart is going to give out—"

"If you girls were that worried, you wouldn't be putting me through this. You'd let me just stay put!"

"—because the doctors say his condition is worse and he could suffer heart failure at any time—"

"—I'm gonna die anyway, just as soon die here at home where I have everything I need!"

"—so we want him to keep the things that he needs but there just isn't room for everything he wants," she ends apologetically.

"Of course," I begin, "this is always difficult—"

"What I want," Charles interrupts yet again but this time physically stepping between his daughter and me, "is for one of you so-called moving professionals to just once try talking to the person this is coming down on. This is my stuff! I'm the one leaving his home and I'm the one who's going to have to do without." He punches a hard finger into his chest and lifts his head defiantly. *Talk to me, don't talk to my daughter!*

Charles was absolutely right. This was all about him. He'd been through an entire morning of others talking about him, picking over his life possessions and making conversation around decisions that directly affected his future—and he simply wanted to be heard. He wanted to remain the decision-maker; he wanted to retain some semblance of control even as he passed control over to his daughters.

Little wonder he was cranky; I've been testy for far less!

Technically the two daughters are my clients since they're footing the bill. And most of the questions I ask during the initial interview directly affect the cost of the move. But my experience has taught me to appreciate with deep understanding that Charles wants to feel empowered, even as he is increasingly powerless. I know how to accomplish this and reassure him. "It's your new home; we will get as much of what is most important to you as we possibly can, but you may have to make some hard choices."

"I can do that," he answers. "Been doing it all my life."

Doesn't that pretty much sum it up for all of us?

Ultimately, I take my time talking him through the decisions he will have to make, deferring to Rose as necessary, but speaking inclusively to him, guiding him through his choices and options, listening to his preferences and the reasons for them, but directing him in a "this or that" manner.

"Nice collection of coats," I say admiringly when we examine the bedroom closet.

"Could be I've been called a dandy a time or two in my day," Charles concedes with a shy grin. "Man can't have too many coats living in New York!"

"That may be, but look at it this way: I'm six feet tall," I explain and stretching my arms out wide. "Think of me as the closet you're going to have, six feet tall by six feet wide—"

Charles eyes me warily.

"—and that's for everything: all your coats, pants, shirts, sweaters, jackets, shoes, hats, belts, scarves, gloves and boots. This is a fine collection of outer wear, but I don't think there's going to be room for it."

"Man's gotta keep warm," Charles counters.

"How about you choose two favorites? One for spring and one for winter? This one's nice," I offer, pulling out a heavy, durable insulated wool jacket. "Hard choices, Charles," I take him in with a steady gaze and a smile. "Only you can make them."

My friendly competitors weren't all that sorry to lose the job to me, Charles not winning the Mister Congeniality Award. But once we'd established his need to be recognized, Charles's manner improved measurably, though not without some grumbling.

Ultimately, Charles was able to keep his queen bed, the piano with all the custom enlarged sheet music his piano teacher had prepared for him, eleven file boxes of teaching aids for his bridge class, and 6' x 6' of tasteful but practical clothes! We eliminated his prized entertainment center, but culled through and repacked his albums, CDs, stereo and television to keep what he most valued. Of course, there were other items, but these were at the root of what he prioritized as a continued source of vitality and happiness for him.

By the time the move was complete, Charles was even smiling!

Rose was smiling too. She was still accomplishing the task of moving a household to a studio space, but arriving there by a path that felt better to her father while staying within their restricted parameters.

He felt better, she felt better, I felt better.

"Talk to me, don't talk to my daughter!" reminded me that even in the throes of taking care of the task at hand as expeditiously and efficiently as possible, special care needs to be taken to make sure everyone feels integrated into the conversation and decisions. Our human desire to be heard and understood does not change or wane with age. Perhaps, because often in our older years we have less social and economic exposure and opportunities to interact, it even becomes all the more imperative.

I believe the greatest gift I can conceive of having from anyone is to be seen by them, heard by them, to be understood and touched by them. The greatest gift I can give is to see, hear, understand and to touch another person. When this is done I feel contact has been made.

—Virginia Satir

CHAPTER TWO

"Always remember—he chose you!"

Edith's life has already been one of loss, so the transition of leaving her home is not unfamiliar to her in the scheme of losses she's already endured. She mentions two miscarriages casually, almost impassively, the first day we begin working together. Jacob, her only surviving child, died of Hodgkins Disease as a young adult. Burt, her husband of thirty-eight years, had passed in his early sixties, leaving her alone now for nearly fifteen years. She is selling the house and moving to assisted living primarily to be closer to her niece Samantha, who lives ninety minutes away and is cheerleading the move for convenience's sake.

Edith is about 5'5" and personifies the modest housewife. She is relatively nondescript—brown hair, brown eyes, average weight, cotton dress, orthopedic shoes, and single gold band on her ring finger. She has above average health with some reduced hearing and vision. If not for proximity to her nearest living relative, she could continue to live in her home for some time. Despite that, though, she seems to bear no unwillingness or animosity toward the move. She appears resigned and is cooperative, helpful and involved in our sorting process—with the exception of Jacob's bedroom.

Jacob was diagnosed with HD when he was twenty and not long thereafter, had to move back to his childhood home for full-time care until his death two years later. His room was cleaned immediately thereafter, but otherwise has remained untouched. Every time I suggested that we start on it, Edith finds other things for us to do. Clearly she is avoiding it. I know the experience is likely to open hurtful memories that have been carefully sealed behind his closed door.

But on the third day, we have systematically sorted through pretty much everything except the master bedroom and Jacob's room. Avoiding it has inadvertently increased the tension and we can no longer put it off.

"You ready for this?" I ask with one hand on the door knob, the other lightly on her shoulder.

"Not really," she smiles ruefully, and then takes a deep breath, leaning against the wall for support. I wait a moment, until she exhales deeply and says, "Okay then."

The room smells stale and slightly sour. First thing, I move to the windows and open them, daylight finding the room for perhaps the first time in thirty years. Edith immediately drops onto the bed and just takes it all in. The room is wallpapered in navy and maroon plaid; there are dark blue linens and comforter on the twin bed, a nightstand with a Star Wars alarm clock, and a small desk with a few framed photos of a blond, blue-eyed boy in various stages of childhood. On the wall over the bed hang a "Saturday Night Fever" poster and a nicely framed senior picture of the same young man with an optimistic grin on his face.

On the up side, there are no pill bottles, bedpans, or wheelchairs—nothing as testimonial to the last months of Jacob's life.

Up until now as we've culled through possessions, I've thrown out options and Edith has made quick decisions. But almost immediately I observe her difficulty in making choices regarding even the simplest items in this room.

"What do you think? Salvation Army?" I ask holding up a beginner's guitar.

"Maybe . . . I don't know. Do you think Samantha might use it one day? I mean, for her children . . . when she has children."

"That could be years from now, a long time to store a guitar, unless you just want to keep it for other reasons..." I hesitate, trying to get a reading on whether the instrument might have some sentimental value because it belonged to her son.

"Jacob got it from a friend and never really got around to playing it much," Edith recalls. "Still, I hate to send it off to just anyone."

"We could ask Samantha. . . ."

"Or we could just give it away. I mean really, it's been here all this time anyway . . . probably isn't worth much. I don't know, what do you think?"

"How about this: I'll bet there are kids at the Scottish Rite Hospital who already play and would love to have a guitar on hand. What about we donate it to them?"

And so I assume a more active role in offering helpful suggestions, trying to minimize the strain on Edith. The longer we're in the room, like Superman too close to Kryptonite, the further Edith sinks into the mattress, clearly losing strength as she struggles to hold it together.

I work as quickly as possible, skip over the small stuff, and get us out of there in less than an hour.

Edith doesn't express a word of hurt or regret or sadness, but when we leave the room, she needs my arm to steady her departure.

When I close the door behind us, she asks, "So we're done with that . . . you can handle the rest, right?"

I assure her I've got it handled and there's absolutely no reason for her to have to revisit the room again. Relieved, exhausted and ready for something a whole lot easier, we head to the master bedroom, the worst of our day behind us.

Or so we think.

The truth is the letters catch us both completely off guard. Facing up to Jacob's room had been an act of necessary bravery and we had every reason to expect the rest of the packing to be innocuous—a kind of unexceptional "reward" for enduring difficult memories and putting the dreaded past behind us. All this is unspoken, of course, but as we begin working together in Edith's bedroom, we are darn near perky—so relieved are we to have Jacob's room behind us.

There is none of the "holding onto the past" surrounding Edith's husband Burt—all his clothing and possessions are long gone and the room is decidedly Edith's. But the room does reflect their years together fondly: on the dresser is a sterling silver framed photo of the two of them on vacation with palm trees in the background and their wedding picture is hanging in a collage of other "him and her" photos on the wall to the left of the bed. In that collection is a matted and framed 30th anniversary greeting card with flowers and glitter and Burt's signature, "My love forever, your Burt".

I assign Edith to the task of sorting through her gloves, scarves, and costume jewelry and she throws herself into the job with due diligence. The chance to be immersed in pretty things is a welcomed change!

I start on the small desk on the wall opposite the bed. I can tell it's been actively used—there are current bills, a checkbook, greeting cards addressed to be mailed but missing stamps. There's stationery with Edith's name on it, the kind you receive as a gift when you donate to certain mail-order charities. There is the requisite desk drawer clutter: rubber bands, paperclips, pen caps, post-it notes, unmatched loose paper, rulers, broken-tip pencils, erasers and dust bunnies.

One drawer is filled with mismatched stationery, three-ring notebook paper, three-by-five notecards, a telephone book and one of those gift calendars you receive from your local hardware store, dated ten years earlier and unused.

I whip through this familiar clutter with the eye of a seasoned pro. But when I remove yet another two phone books from the bottom and final desk drawer, I spot a bundle of letters, held together by two fat rubber bands, hidden behind them and stuffed at the back. The envelopes are time-worn and faded, the writing cursive. The postal stamp date on the top letter is 1946.

"Edith, what are these old letters?" I ask spontaneously.

But Edith is caught up in her task, smiles absentmindedly and keeps on sorting.

I unwrap the bundle, read the addressee and say again, "Edith, it looks like there are letters here that belong to your husband."

"Could be, that used to be his desk," Edith responds casually, weighing her choices between a nice blue paisley scarf and one very similar but in green.

I remove the letter from the top envelope and begin to read aloud.

"Dear Burt, I hope you remember me, I know I have thought of you so many times since you were here in Germany—"

I stop mid-sentence, look at Edith, who has stopped mid-task, giving me her full attention. Gently, I move to the bed and sit beside her. "It looks like these letters were written to your husband—why don't we have a look at them together, okay?"

Edith nods but doesn't opt to read along with me. Instead, she fixes her gaze off into a corner of the room as I continue. I read, "I don't think I will ever forget the time we spent together. Your buddies were so very funny and my girlfriends and I laughed so much and we are still laughing just remembering all the fun!"

I hesitate, but there's really no other option than to continue. Since there's no rule in the handbook for situations like this, I'm operating purely on intuition and compassion. I read slowly and without censure.

The letter goes on to reference, in fairly innocent detail, a night between a group of American soldiers, including Burt, and the local girls, where at least one of the women—the sender—took the evening to heart. It ends, "I would like it if you could come back here again. I have such fondness for you, and it seemed like you did for me. I think we could make a life together and be very happy, don't you? Please write soon and tell me you feel the same way."

The letter is signed, "love, Anneken."

I finish with zero intention of reading any of the other half a dozen or so letters that follow.

The silence that follows is heart-wrenching. Edith continues to stare off into the corner of the room, her eyes distant and distracted. I imagine her watching a replay of the past five decades of her life. The blue and green paisley scarves, now clutched in a tight wad in her lap, are telling.

I reach over and untangle one hand from her lap and hold it between both of mine. When I do, her head turns and she registers me as if surprised I am there. "Edith," I say gently, *"Always remember—he chose you!"*

When I spoke those words, I saw Edith's face wash with relief. Just the same way as I had engaged more actively in Jacob's room to facilitate an emotionally charged process, I was volunteering a way for her to assimilate this new, unexpected piece of information about her husband's life in a way that might help keep her memories and perspective of her marriage intact. My words were instinctual, giving her a path to make sense of the letters without having to forage into her past and second guess the legitimacy of what she shared over a lifetime with Burt.

And they were words from my heart and what I believe was truth: the bottom line is that Burt did choose Edith and they created a family and a lifetime together. The letters confronted Edith with a pivotal moment of, "What am I supposed to do with this information?"—and I knew any attempt to dissect it further, to reach into the past and try to analyze or reconstruct, would have been destructive and self-defeating.

In this case, the physical move from her home was very much about coming to peace with the past and moving forward with a cleansed heart. We thought it was about making peace with the memories of Jacob and discovered it was also about choosing peace with her husband.

In other hands, this scenario could have played out half a dozen different ways. A joke could have fueled further antagonism between the sexes: "Isn't that just like a man? Wouldn't you know? Can't trust them as far as you can throw them! I knew this guy who . . . ."

It could have degraded into a reality television moment: "Edith, how does this make you feel? Do you think your husband loved another woman all these years? Is it possible there could have been an 'Anneken' reunion . . . ."

It could have deteriorated into a bitter indictment against marriage in general: "You think this is bad? I knew a woman whose husband . . . ."

But the practical reality is that Edith really had no one with whom she could have explored the implications of the letters, even if it had gone drama's way. Edith's relationship with her niece was cordial but far from intimate. And at this point in her life, there really was no one else.

My gift to Edith was to diffuse the content of the letter before it had a chance to grab her heart and plant seeds of doubt and confusion that would grow and poison her memories in the years ahead. As soon as I said the words, I knew I had done the right thing.

Each of us has stories that others don't know. Expect that in times of transition, some of those stories will find their way to the light. Our challenge is to handle them—ourselves or on behalf of others—with kindness and the benefit of doubt; to release them without attachment, second guessing or a "need to know".

Three things in human life are important:
the first is to be kind; the second is to be kind;
and the third is to be kind.

—Henry James

CHAPTER THREE

"I can still see the photographs in my mind!"

Eunice and Bernice are sisters in their mid-eighties. They are both exactly the same height—5'6"—and seem to take pleasure and pride in the telling of it. But any similarity stops there.

Eunice has a sturdy build and is unadorned in a dark cotton shift and low rise work boots. Her features are strong and plain, her white hair cut straight at the jawline. She has a quick smile, a strong voice, and large masculine hands that help her feel her way around the house: she's legally blind and has been for the last seven years. She doesn't wear corrective lenses or dark glasses, has only slightly cloudy gray eyes and moves her body and head during conversations in such a way that you might not know she was blind at all. Eunice is the older sister and has the more dominant, authoritative role between sisters.

Bernice, on the other hand, looks like a strong wind could blow her away. She's not scrawny, just slight and filled with nervous energy that keeps her fussing about, never really settling. She still drives and runs most of the house errands and does the shopping. Since she gets out in the community, she is more attentive to her appearance. She wears colorful pant sets or skirts and sweaters and likes dangling earrings and bangle bracelets. Her features are softer than her sister's, but she has the same quick smile and a lyrical, playful voice—she likes to tease Eunice and Eunice likes to pretend to complain about it.

Both women are widowed and share the house that Eunice and her husband Ephram lived in together for 42 years. Years ago when Eunice could no longer manage alone with her vision loss, Bernice, already widowed, sold her own home and moved in. Now the two of them are moving to an independent condo with a full-time health support. Eunice's son Peter has stepped in to facilitate the decision, which puts his mother and aunt minutes away from where he and his wife and children live. He has hired us to handle the details of the move and I anticipate it will be a reasonably uncomplicated event—inasmuch as moving from 2,800 square foot home to 1,000 square foot condo can be!

Bernice and I, working as a team, become a verbal duet— broadcasting descriptions of items to Eunice as she readily hands out decisions for distribution. Since Bernice let most of her own things go when she moved in, the majority of the possessions in the house are from Eunice's life with Ephram. So Bernice is content to defer to Eunice—her older sister sorting through the details of her life, the younger providing lighthearted commentary.

"Those were our mother's dishes," Eunice responds when I describe some English fine bone china in vintage pink roses. "They have to come with us."

"I wanted these dishes myself, you know," Bernice teases. "Mother always liked you best."

"Don't be silly," Eunice counters. "She gave you that beautiful Royal Doulton set with the pale blue border—don't you remember? The pink and yellow and blue flowers?"

"Of course I remember," Bernice answers. "But this was my favorite. And hers. And look who got them!"

"Well, we both have them now so get over it," Eunice dismisses gruffly, but the curve of a smile on her lips betrays she is enjoying the banter—or enjoying the memory of besting her sister!

"I think a set of four should be plenty," I volunteer. "How about we put aside the others to pass along as an eight-piece set?"

"Oh look, Eunice! What in the world are these doing in the china cabinet?" Bernice pulls out three large white gift boxes and sets them one-by-one on the dining room table we're using as our work area. "It's your pin cushions!"

She gleefully opens the lids to reveal dozens and dozens of tissue wrapped balls. She unwraps one and says, "It's a whale!"

Eunice reaches for it and Bernice places it into her hands. "Gray ceramic," Eunice murmurs, feeling the cushion with probing fingers. "Soft blue cushion back, says 'North to the Future' right here on the underside," as she rubs the whale's belly.

"Exactly!" Bernice applauds with delight.

"Ephram and I picked this up in Alaska back in '77—"

There are over a hundred pin-cushions from around the world; we agree to whittle the collection to forty. It could be a tedious assignment, but Eunice remembers each one in detail as she appreciatively handles them and Bernice takes as much pleasure watching her sister as looking through the pin cushions themselves. We spend the necessary time to look at them one-by-one and I am pleasantly surprised by Eunice's uncanny memory—and will be surprised again and again throughout the course of the day.

Later, in the guest bedroom, I discover the closets and drawers are jam-packed with fabric yardage—a collection of material used over the years for dresses, quilts and crafts. Bernice and Eunice were seamstresses during the war and share a love of fabrics that has endured over the years. There are swatches and yards of material in every imaginable color and texture, and each one has a story they are delighted to recollect!

I pull out a deep green cotton print, thinking it's another measure of fabric and Bernice gasps. "My dress!"

She stands with the dress pressed against her torso and whirls. "Eunice, it's the dress I made for the World's Fair!"

Then she dips down, rummages around in the contents of the drawer and comes up with another one in dark blue, holding it up in the other hand like a prize. "Yours is here too! Do you remember, Eunice? Remember making them special?"

"In 1964—how could I forget!" she answers, taking hers into lap, smelling the dress, feeling the buttons and the collar. "We didn't decide until last minute to make them and were up half the night finishing them up. You were still stitching your hem on the train to Queens!"

This grabs my attention because the '64 New York World's Fair at Flushing Meadows Corona Park in the borough of Queens was an event I also attended! I was twelve and flew in from San Diego eager to experience a glimpse of the future as revealed by industrial exhibitors like General Motors, IBM Corporation and Bell Systems.

Bernice has moved to a mirror and is admiring the dress against her torso. "We wanted to look extra special . . ."

". . . and we did!" Eunice mused. "Remember how our husbands claimed that we were the most stylish girls there? They surprised us with corsages, roses of all things. . . ."

"Remember they teased us that they bought them so they wouldn't lose us in the crowds—the two prettiest girls with the fanciest dresses, wearing flowers that left a perfumed trail everywhere we went!"

For a brief moment, the three of us silently recall our own fond memories from 1964.

"We need to keep the dresses," Bernice pronounces happily. "So what if they don't fit anymore?"

"Absolutely," Eunice agrees. "The dresses come with us!"

Who am I to argue? I still have the souvenirs from that trip myself! One day, my son—or someone providing a service like mine—may be asking me, too, if the 1964 World's Fair mementos are really that important.

Later, we split up the "tripping down memory lane" team and Bernice goes to organize her own room. Eunice and I tackle hers. Most of Ephram's possessions are gone, but occasionally we run into something and we give it instant assignment to charity. In one drawer of cotton panties and nylon stockings, I find a black wool sock.

"Check the toe. Has it been darned?" Eunice asks.

"Sure enough," I answer, finding the neat rows of stitches. "Like a pro."

"That's Ephram's. Guess I never got around to giving it back to him," she chuckles.

You might think someone totally blind would go out of their way to minimalize decorations, accessories and floor objects—things that can be bumped, broken or send you plummeting. But Eunice's home has all the clutter and chaos of a sighted one. So it takes us a while to do the "verbalize-sort" process through all her clothing, scarves, costume jewelry, perfume bottles, knick-knacks and collectibles. We've got it going though, and we're making good time.

I have trouble getting the bottom dresser door open; it's heavy and takes both hands and a good, solid yank. It's stuffed with photo albums, the old fashioned kind with the pictures inset with stays glued to heavy paper. There are at least half a dozen of them: thick, dusty and bulging.

"I guess there's no reason to keep those," Eunice volunteers in response to my explanation of what I've found.

I open one and see a polaroid photo of five children dancing in water spewing from a fire hydrant. I describe it.

"Oh, that's Bernice and me with the kids in the neighborhood," Eunice answers, reaching out to find the album and drawing it into her own lap. Her fingers move around the page until remarkably, she finds the precise photo we're discussing. "Brooklyn, we weren't more than seven or eight . . . well, I was probably seven, Bernice was five. One of those kids, the one with pigtails—her name was Martha and the three of us were the best of friends. We went everywhere together right up until high school graduation. Just the sweetest girl you ever met. She got married to a boy, Tony, who was killed in the war. Isn't there a tow-headed boy in the picture?"

"The one laying on his stomach in the street?" I ask, taking a seat next to her so I can get a better view.

"That's the one," she laughs. "He was pretending to be a shark! My uncle was photographing us and David just had to show off. That boy loved attention, and loved the girls—got into some trouble later and joined the army. He made it through but I never heard what happened to him. By then Ephram and I had moved to Long Island. . . ."

One picture leads to another, Eunice utilizing touch and feel to recall each photo and relay the stories behind it.

"Well, that's enough about that," Eunice laughs a little self-consciously when we've revisited the five on the page. "I don't suppose those old photos are going to do anybody any good. Don't know who would want them though. . . ."

"Why don't we take a minute," I suggest, "and just have a look through these?"

"Don't be silly," Eunice objects. "There must be hundreds of pictures in those books. You surely don't have the time for that—and what good would it do?"

"I think we can make time if you're up for it," I answer.

"Well, I suppose it might be nice to have a look," she admits and turns the page to feel for the next photo.

I pull the chair closer and get comfortable.

"Isn't it funny?" Eunice wonders out loud. *"I can still see the photographs in my mind!"*

Nearly two hours later, I know in my heart that Eunice has "seen" her photo collection for the last time. Even though she and Bernice decide to make room for the albums in their new condo, I know they'll mostly collect dust or be hidden away until their home is dismantled a final time. Occasionally an album may be dragged out during family get-togethers to look at one picture or a few. But never again would Eunice be given the time, opportunity and audience to revisit them in a way that was as meaningful and comprehensive as what we did that day.

My experience with Eunice helped me recognize the subtle impact that impairments can have in our relationships with the adult aging. If I have a parent who no longer hears well, I may be tempted to engage them less often in conversation; our communication may be reduced to one-sentence exchanges because it's draining on both of us to try. If my parent is less mobile, it may become easier to limit the number of trips out of the house, taper off the walks outside, minimize their activity within the home. If my parent has difficulty speaking, does that mean they have less to say?

Dealing with impairments requires extra effort, patience, tolerance and acceptance for all those involved. Dealing with impairments requires love, compassionate understanding and kindness.

Eunice's vision had been gone for seven years and undoubtedly had been progressively worsening for many years before that. But blindness had not robbed her of visual images on the movie screen in her mind—and in fact, her keen recollection of detail may even have been a repercussion of her vision loss. She exhibited uncanny "vision" when we took time to facilitate it—in this case because it was necessary for the move. But in the years ahead, when again would she have the opportunity to "see" as she had done that day?

"I can still see the photographs in my mind!" reminded me that even while those we love may suffer the physical impairments of aging, their hearts and minds still call out for consideration. The desire for expression of our selves—through thoughts, opinions or memories—doesn't change with age or impairment, but may take more deliberate intention on the part of those around us to facilitate.

The worst part of holding memories is not the pain.
It's the loneliness of it. Memories need to be shared.

— Lois Lowry

CHAPTER FOUR

"Hide the painting in the elevator— my brother's coming!"

The Long Island Gold Coast is an opulent section of Long Island's North Shore region that was popularized as the setting of the Redford version of 'The Great Gatsby'. Our client's home is one of the mansions that grace this scenic coastal area. Unlike most towering "castle-like" estates though, it has a one level, ranch-style layout consisting of eleven rooms and a three-car garage. Its only elevator is off the kitchen and travels to the basement—a large room that what at one time may have been a servant's dining quarters.

Our role is relatively simple compared to other moves. The mother, and home owner, is staying with friends during the transition so we have no emotional maneuvering resulting from her attendance. Too, the delegation of possessions between siblings, assisted living, charities and auction houses has been carefully discussed, agreed upon and detailed in writing prior to our arrival. The packing and moving process is being supervised by the two daughters: Deborah is overseeing the crews from Sotheby's and Christie's; Susan is managing our team, sorting through and packing everything else.

I am surprised to receive a phone call from Lou, my team leader in charge of the project.

"Calling in the reserves," he states matter-of-factly. "We're not going to make deadline."

"What's the problem?" I ask.

"No problem on our end. But they just accepted an offer on the sale of the house—mansion, palace, whatever you call this place—and upped our time frame by a week. We're going to need more arms and legs."

I make the necessary changes to our schedule and arrive the next morning with two more of our staff, Angela and Saul, prepared for exacting but uneventful labor.

There is organized chaos everywhere. Four, 18-wheel moving trucks are parked back-to-back in the circular drive and workers are scurrying around like ants, the sisters at the center of the frenzy. Deborah and Susan could be twins: both in their forties, trim, wispy blond hair, cultured smiles and suitably attired in an upscale variation of moving grubs: Hilfiger khaki slacks, LaCoste polos, and Fendi loafers. They are a model of efficacy, working from clipboards bursting with diagrams, lists, estimates and appraisals.

Deborah has set up base of operations out of the formal dining room. Her team is packing items of value—silver, antiques, rugs, clocks, lamps, wine and art—that will be sold at auction. Wood crates are being carefully filled with treasures, and the echo of drills and hammers sealing them for shipment is lost in the whirlwind of activity.

Our group is working with Susan from the parlor. She relegates items based on her own clipboard and knows what will be donated, discarded or distributed between the three siblings. John, their brother, is not present but has his own assignment of possessions, like his sisters. Whenever there's a question about where something goes, Susan consults the clipboard and quickly finds the answer.

I send Angela to the kitchen, where there are half a dozen, twelve-piece sets of formal china waiting to be packed. She's never done a kitchen before, so I demonstrate the packing process with the first set, showing her how, contrary to popular practice, to set the plates in the packing boxes on their edges rather than lying flat. Susan has provided us with a photo illustration of each pattern and to whom the set is assigned and in no time at all, Angela is knee deep in soup bowls and server sets. I rejoin the rest of our team, now six in number, in the parlor.

Our foremost concern during a move is speed. Our clients are paying by the hour and we've provided an estimate of the number of hours we believe the job will take. Any hours that exceed that estimate invite customer concern and/or dissatisfaction and necessitate explanation, justification and conversation. Over the years, I've learned it's just easier and better business to stay on schedule. So we work fast, stay focused and don't chat about the weather.

When a move is well-planned and on-track, there's a kind of camaraderie that builds as everyone knows their role and works in tandem. This is one of those times and the dozen or so of us movers operate like machinery, heads buried in a comfortable flow of coordinated turmoil. Susan is doing an admirable job keeping things moving and maintaining a composed, perhaps even valiant, disposition and competency.

Lou is in one of the two living rooms, just adjacent to the parlor, rolling area rugs that are too worn to be of resale value. As I join him after relegating assignments in the kitchen, I see Susan step out of sight into the hall, apparently taking a phone call where it's a bit quieter. I've just stooped to help Lou when she bursts back into the room, all color drained from her face, a blond curl suddenly out of place and flopping into her now wide and alarmed eyes. She frantically points past us and, in a voice that shrieks above the static of a dozen movers and commotion, cries out, *"Hide the painting in the elevator—my brother's coming!"*

In the following seconds of stunned silence, no one moves. "The painting, the painting!" she repeats, stabbing her pointed finger in our direction. "We've got to get it out of here. Quick—to the elevator!"

Lou and I regain our composure and jump to the ready, following the angle of her directive to an object as big as the wall itself. It's an oil painting of dogs and horses and a fox running for dear life and it's big—at least five-by seven feet. With a ten-inch, ornate, gilded frame adding to its girth, it doesn't invite being moved now—or ever. But Susan is waving at us to follow her and she's already halfway across the room. There's no time to make a plan or strategize on the best way to carry it, so Lou just shrugs and we latch on wherever we can and start penguin walking rapidly in the same direction as Susan is running. We scuttle around dining tables, half-open crates, packing materials scattered about the floor and workers who get out of our way. We forge corners with haste and just enough expertise not to bang into walls or fall flat on our faces. Susan is running interference ahead of us, frantically identifying obstacles in our path, while commanding us to "Hurry!"

Just as we arrive at the service elevator—four rooms and a half a football field later—we hear the front door clatter from the other side of the house and a man's muffled voice cry, "For God's sake!"

Susan flinches, then hisses, "Take it downstairs and wait!" and scurries away.

Now Lou and I become a "Mutt and Jeff" act trying to jam the mammoth painting into an elevator designed for serving carts. Somehow we do it, but to this day, I couldn't say how. What I remember most vividly is the image of Lou wrapped around the painting like an octopus, utilizing every body part to hold the ponderous thing in balance. As the doors close upon him, I yelp, "Don't come up until I call you!"

Then I return to the parlor and take Lou's place folding rugs just as if nothing had happened.

But a tornado has hit the household and shattered our machine-like efficiency. John, the brother and son, is just a little guy, shorter and slighter than his sisters; the same blonde hair but wearing a Brooks Brothers pinstripe suit and Cole Haan wingtips. He is a little guy, but one with a big attitude—a bad one. He's launched into the room and is spitting out challenges and complaints like a tommy gun, not even bothering to wait for answers: "What's this doing here? I thought it was going with Mom. Where's the match to this? Isn't this a set? Why is this in this box? Isn't it Deborah's?"

And, throwing a dismissive wave around the room to include everyone but him, "Do these people even know what they're doing? We'll never find anything in this mess!"

Deborah has joined her sister and the two of them are tagging alongside John with equal parts apology, frustration and something "sibling". They seem to be trying to appease him with answers while simultaneously trying to steer him out of the working area. I see Susan lay a hand on his arm to guide him away and he bats her off brusquely, picks up a music box from the table and says, "I remember this! We can't give this up to strangers!"

When he charges into the kitchen, I follow—fearful of leaving Angela unprotected in the storm. Sure enough: "Excuse me, but where's the blue set? I thought I was supposed to get the blue set! What's happened to it? Where's my blue set of dishes?"

It takes an orchestrated effort, but moments later, John is being firmly but gently escorted into the garden by his sisters, one on each arm, both talking in low voices to their brother, who seems to have spent his energy and has assumed the air of a sheepish little boy. They stay outside, quietly talking, and just as the crew begins to regain its momentum, John noiselessly re-enters the house, winds his way to the front door and departs.

Just before exiting, he says "Keep up the good work" to two guys carrying an antique buffet, pausing to give him right of way.

The entire group heaves a collective sigh of relief, but, undaunted, immediately sets back to work. So lulled by disaster averted, I am ten minutes into the next project before I suddenly gasp and take off at a run. I have completely forgotten Lou and the painting! I speed dial his phone and arrive just as the emerging elevator appears.

The doors open and there's Lou, red-faced and sweaty, still balancing the painting for dear life.

"All in a day's work," my team leader grins.

And with that, Lou and I set about getting the monster thing back out of the elevator.

I have no idea what was going on with John that day or why a painting had to be hustled away to the basement as if to protect it from evil forces beyond our control. Susan did not volunteer an explanation so in the retelling, we've created our own: Susan was pirating the painting to finance her next trip to the French Riviera; there had been a knock-down, drag-out fight over the piece the night before and Susan and Deborah didn't have any rounds left to step into the ring again; sibling rivalry, boys against the girls, had reared it's evil head and we bore witness.

What I do know is that this move was exemplary in every way—rarely have I seen such a clear delineation of and absence of emotional charge over possessions. More often, there is high drama and a stage that reveals sibling rivalry, jealousy, pettiness, anger, and resentment. Sometimes these feelings are new ones born from the move itself, but more often they mirror unresolved issues dating back as far as childhood.

This was a move founded on the best of intentions: the siblings had worked together and by all appearances, had completed their negotiations and reached agreements that were signed and in writing.

Maybe John had a fight with his wife that morning and needed an outlet. Maybe a critical deal fell through at work or someone cut him off in traffic or the Starbucks line took longer than he planned. Maybe he got up that morning and suddenly felt the weight of losing the home he grew up in or panicked to know his mother was entering a new, next phase of her life experience. Maybe Mercury was in retrograde and this was going to be a bad day no matter what happened.

John arrived looking for a fight and unique to my experiences, his sisters didn't give it to him. Somehow love prevailed and they were able to say what was needed to ease his panic and leave him with sufficient dignity and grace to exit with an encouraging word to those he had criticized moments before.

If this model family was susceptible to the sudden, unexpected emotional disruption, then most of us will be, too. *"Hide the painting in the elevator—my brother's coming!"* is a reminder to expect the unexpected during the emotionally charged dissolution of a home, its possessions and its memories. Conflict can arise within already strained sibling relationships. Or, what triggers the participants can come from left field and may be completely unrelated to anything about the move itself.

By expecting the unexpected, by anticipating that the dismantling of a home will be fraught with emotional charges, you can be thinking about "escape plans" and how you might handle worst case scenarios if they should happen. I've had clients rehearse and practice their responses to imagined scenarios, especially when there are predictable fragile personal relationships in the mix. It may sound arbitrary, but creatively anticipating where hurt feelings might reveal themselves and agreeing on what action to take is a proven way to avoid disruption of the moving process and/or creating lingering or permanent chasms between family members.

Expect the best, plan for the worst,
and prepare to be surprised.

—Denis Waitley

Chapter Five

"So the kids don't want our stuff—now what?"

When Howard suffered a stroke two months earlier, he sustained no permanent paralysis but it was clear he would never fully recover his strength and vitality. After the stroke, he exhibited periods of confusion and uncertainty that were uncharacteristic of him. He slept more, suffered mood swings and bouts of depression.

It was difficult to assess how much of the emotional and intellectual symptoms were related the immediate physical trauma on his system and might eventually pass, but Natalie, his wife acted without reservations. She quickly made the decision for them both to move to assisted living where Howard could be under 24-hour medical supervision and contacted me to help. As Natalie expressed it, "Honey, how we spend the rest of our lives together is way more important than where—worrying about Howard isn't how I want to spend it."

I met Natalie while Howard was still in rehab regaining some impaired muscle control on his right side. She was bright and articulate and sharply dressed in traditional designer clothes, had stylish gray hair, alert blue eyes and a knowing smile.

She told me that when Howard was ready to be released, she wanted him to go directly to their new apartment so that the emotional trauma related to moving would be minimized. So the move happened quickly. She and I did a walk-through of their three-bedroom home and she coolly chose what she wanted to take, and easily parted with things she recognized had little value to anyone—those items that just seem to accumulate in closets and storage areas over the many years in a home. We sent more than a dozen boxes to Goodwill and parted with assurances that we would meet again in a few weeks to work out the remaining items with her two sons.

""I want the apartment to look and feel as much like the home he left six weeks ago as possible. It's more important to me to fill the new apartment with memories and knick knacks we've collected together over the years than holding onto the family heirlooms." After making her selections, she expressed confidence that her sons could make use of any number of valued items she was forced to leave behind.

"Let's just hope it doesn't come to fist fights," she joked as we made our rounds through the house identifying what would go and what would stay.

Because Howard had done measurably well in insurance for fifty years, they'd been fortunate to travel. During numerous trips to Israel, they had collected items that they particularly held dear: a set of brass Sabbath candlesticks; a Seder brass Passover tray; an assortment of fine art statues and figurines made by Israeli artists; a handmade stone and clay menorah; a print of Sandra Silberzweig's *Hamsa Blessings*; and several framed tapestries.

"It may seem like a lot for one small apartment," Natalie conceded somewhat guiltily, "but I want this move to be as effortless for Howard as possible. He's so very fond of the travel we've done together and I just know having these things around him will give him comfort."

I assured her there was sufficient room for her treasures but limited room for any additional things she might want to keep when we returned to sort through everything else.

"I'm not worried about it," she answered. "It's just stuff and I'd rather the boys have most of it anyway."

We took her Jasperware collection with the understanding it might have to take second place to her other treasures. And this was one of those occasions when I conceded room for two sets of dishes—kosher and trefah. She also chose to have the custom draperies from both the living room and the master bedroom cleaned and reinstalled in their new apartment.

There was a lot left in the house for later reckoning.

Now six weeks later, I am at the house with Howard and Natalie to finish the job. Natalie has invited their two sons to meet us here to go through everything they left behind and set aside what they'd like to keep for their own homes. While we wait, and as often happens when I am in the company of those preparing to leave their home, Natalie idly browses through the living room where we are seated and reminisces about various items and the memories they trigger about their lives together and as parents.

"You remember, Howard, when Tyler took thirteen stitches off the corner of this end table when he was seven?" she asks fondly, her hand caressing a mahogany console.

"He was the fiercest of pirates," Howard chuckles.

They share a moment and then Natalie adds, "We were lucky that old hourglass lamp held together and didn't add to his wounds."

There's a knock at the door in the same moment and the "pirate" in question arrives with his wife Hannah. Tyler is the oldest son, married to his high school sweetheart, and father to a boy and a girl. He has followed his father's footsteps in insurance and has agencies in three states including New York. He and Hannah live in a five-bedroom home on the Lower East Side.

"We were just talking about you!" Natalie exclaims and repeats the memory, in greater detail, for their benefit.

Tyler smiles indulgently, but says, "We're good here for only a couple of hours, Mom. The neighborhood has a barbeque thing going on this afternoon, so we need to get this done in pretty short order. Shouldn't take long anyway, should it?"

Steven, the younger son, arrives then almost as if on cue. He's driven from his house on Long Island. Although equally as successful as his brother, he first had to overcome drug and alcohol abuse that at its climax, left him living on the streets. Now a survivor of those experiences, he owns a group of drug treatment centers in Lower Manhattan. With him is Kathy, his girlfriend of eighteen months, and who serves as the CFO of his businesses.

I've had many experiences when the offspring of the adult making the move are heavily invested in acquiring possessions from the home being vacated. This is not one of them. From the beginning, both boys and their partners appear to be largely perfunctory about the process and seem to have little interest in collecting items from Howard and Natalie's home.

We get started immediately, focusing on the larger furnishings first, and well into our second hour, no one has claimed a single piece of furniture, not the least of which a beautiful, mahogany antique dining room table and chairs handed down to Natalie from her mother.

"I'm sure the set is valuable," Natalie insists.

"Then sell it, Mother, and put aside the money for yourselves," Tyler responds.

"But they've been in our family for three generations," she pursues.

"Mom, I really don't have a place for them," Steven says. "And even if I did, the style is all wrong."

"We already have our own second set in storage from the last house we lived in before we bought this one," Hannah says. "Tyler and I hate to give it up and keep thinking we might use it one day, but we never do. The same thing would happen if we took yours. Wouldn't you rather it goes to someone who really needs it?"

"I'd rather keep it in the family," Natalie says.

"What about the grandkids?" Howard suggests to Tyler.

"Dad, they're in middle school."

"So tell them it's a family heirloom, something they can fight over when they grow up," Howard answers.

"I don't think so, Dad," Tyler says. "It's another dozen years before they'll even be thinking about setting up a home and by that time, we'll have paid ten times the value in storage fees."

"Maybe we could store it for you until they're ready," Natalie suggests.

This gets a definitive "no" from all three men. She sighs heavily but lets it go.

It's crowded in the bedroom that used to be Steven's. Natalie is seated at the end of the double bed and Howard is leaning against the headboard. Tyler is examining school photos hanging on the wall and in frames on the bookshelf and pointing out Steven and himself to the women.

"Take that graduation photo, Steven," Natalie says pointing to a framed, sepia 8" x 10" hanging on the wall. "It would look perfect in your office."

"Naw, that's okay, Mom," Steven laughs. "I'd be more likely to put it in the garden to scare away the crows."

"Ditto that," Tyler agrees and they laugh.

"Take all those photos, why don't you," Natalie adds, waving her hand toward a collection on the bookshelf.

"What would I do with them?" Steven asks. "You keep them, Mom."

"Honey, we don't have enough wall space and almost no shelf space," Natalie says. "And besides, I didn't graduate, you did."

"Barely," Steven admits. "Not a lot of fond memories from those days."

"Probably not a lot of memories period," Tyler observes rather wryly, but Steven nods in brotherly agreement.

"Don't we have some of these same photos in an album at home?" Hannah asks her husband. "They look a little familiar."

"Probably," Tyler answers. "Look, Mom, we didn't really come here to add to the stuff we already have in the attic. All these photos from when we were kids? They're here for you and Dad."

"And we've enjoyed them. But now that we've moving, they should get handed down to you boys."

"Mom, to be honest, old photos just don't do that much for me," Steven admits. "If you and Dad don't have a place for them, tossing them is okay with me."

"Ditto that," Tyler says again.

Natalie stares at her sons in disbelief. Howard seems to be catching a cat nap and is missing the debate. "I can't just throw them away," she says.

"Sure you can," Tyler says and scoops up a handful of frames from the shelf and drops them into a waste basket. He and Steven high-five and that ends the discussion.

When we hit the garage, Howard is the one attempting charm and coercion.

"These are perfectly good tools—it's not like tools wear out!" he says.

"But we have our own tools," Tyler answers.

"Or we have our own handyman who has his own tools," Steven amends.

"Actually, we have both—our own tools and a handyman on twenty-four hour speed dial. And we still go out a buy new whenever something breaks," Hannah says.

"Could be the guys at one of our treatment centers would be able to use them when they get out," Kathy suggests.

"What about the grandkids?" Howard persists.

"Lisa and Mark wouldn't know a tool if it hit them on the side of the head," Tyler admits.

"Let alone know what to do with it if it did," Hannah adds.

"Sometimes they apply for jobs that require their own set of tools," Kathy explains.

"I know you don't like hearing this, Mom and Dad, but I don't plan on having kids. No kids, so no tools," Steven says with some relief.

"I taught you how to use a hammer and screwdriver when you were just a boy—what's wrong with you, Tyler?"

"They're not interested, Dad," Tyler defends. "Kids today don't want to use their hands for anything but texting."

"A good set of tools could be the ticket to help a clean addict start his life over again," Kathy persists.

"I'm leaving this up to you boys and your dad," Natalie weighs in, "but I have to agree, it would be nice if the tools stayed in the family."

"Versus someone actually using them?" Steven says. "I'm with Kathy; let's donate them to the treatment center for some kid trying to get a new start."

"I just hate to waste them on some stranger," Howard says.

"It could change a life," Kathy encourages.

"Oh all right," Howard concedes irritably. "You don't have to go on and on about it. I heard you the first time."

When it's all said and done that day, not much changes hands between the generations. Tyler claims a desk lamp from his father's office; Hannah picks up some table linens and placemats; Steven volunteers to take some of the board games they played as children, once again for the drug treatment center; and Kathy scores with both the tools and the riding lawn mower, also for the center.

"Better to give this stuff to people who can really appreciate it," Tyler says by way of goodbye. "But thanks, Mom and Dad, for thinking of us!"

"Think of it as a good thing," Steven asserts. "Your children love you, not your stuff—how many parents can lay claim to that?"

As soon as the door closes after them, Natalie turns to her husband and says, "Well, that was a waste of time."

"I thought we raised them better," Howard sighs.

"No respect for the past is the problem," Natalie laments.

"What's the world coming to?" Howard shakes his head in dismay.

Natalie looks at me helplessly. *"So the kids don't want our stuff—now what?"*

During the arduous task of dismantling a home, there is no equation for the value children will place on the items within it. I've seen siblings nearly come to blows over everyday objects one could find at the local thrift store. I've also seen valuable treasures go unclaimed and donated to charity. In this case, money was not an issue for Tyler or Steven and the $4,200 we got for the antique dining set was incidental to them. But in the majority of families with whom I've worked, the perceived or actual dollar value plays a fundamental role as possessions are divided. In most cases, there is a calculated effort within families to disperse items equally, "fairly". Often there is at least one adult child who has less income or greater need than the other siblings. Sometimes the other siblings yield to that need, sometimes they don't. Tensions can mount and conflicts erupt regardless of which way it goes.

But frequently there is an emotional attachment assigned to items by aging adults leaving their home that their children may not consider. Howard and Natalie had years of memories associated with the dining room set—fused to years of memories by family before them. And what parent doesn't re-experience memories of their child growing up when looking at photos and want that child to feel the same way when they view them? I have no doubt that when Howard contemplated his tools, he revisited the projects he worked on with his sons when they were young and felt the memories of the time they spent together.

Handing these items over to their children allows the parents to perpetuate memories; it seems to validate the parent-child connection; and it allows the parents to experience a sense of well-being about the life they're leaving behind. When a child ignores or disregards the emotional connection parents have to their personal possessions, it can feel like a violation.

By the same token, adult children want what they want.

"So the kids don't want our stuff—now what?" invites us to remember that the belongings contained within the four walls of a home have both a material and an emotional value; and that if items are relegated out of the family, it be handled with gentle regard that honors the memories attached.

What does a man possess if not for the memories
left behind after he has departed?
—Benjamin M. Strozykowski

Chapter Six

"I just tripped over my slippers— what's the big deal?"

"Well, you just can't imagine how panicked I was," says Barbara. "It wasn't just the fall—not that it wasn't enough of a fright! He had blood gushing from a cut on his forehead and it was getting all over the place—"

"A head wound bleeds a lot, Mom, even when it's not life-threatening," volunteers her son David.

"And how exactly is a person supposed to know?" Barbara demands. "It looked critical to me—"

"I'm not criticizing, Mom—"

"I was okay," says Steve, the husband/father whose fall set the current plan into action. "I just needed a minute to get up—"

"You couldn't get up!" insisted Barbara. "You were too disoriented. You weren't making any sense at all!"

"I would have made it up eventually. And I would have started making sense; I just needed a minute to regroup."

"You needed my help and you know it. And the way you landed all twisted and bent around the toilet and squeezed next to the vanity—I couldn't get a good grip, especially with all the blood—"

"Mom, you did the right thing calling '911'—"

"Tell your father that!"

"I have told dad that," David insists. "Dad," he says, turning to Steve, "Mom did the right thing calling for help."

"I'm just saying we could have saved a lot of trouble if she'd just given me a minute—"

"How many minutes, exactly, Steven?" Barbara asks her husband. "How many minutes before you bled to death? Or your heart gave out? Just how long was I supposed to let you lay there without help?"

"Well, a cold compress for my head might have helped—"

"A cold compress? I'm supposed to hand over a bag of ice and just let you lay there not knowing if you've broken your hip or fractured an ankle or if you've got a concussion—"

"You could have asked me my name," Steve insists. "Isn't that what they do to check for a concussion?"

"And how was I supposed to check for a broken hip—ask you to march around the room?"

"Mom, we know Dad couldn't have marched—"

"Of course he couldn't—he couldn't even sit up! That's my point, he was lying there on the floor and he was too big and too heavy and in such an awkward position—"

"I'm not so big and heavy," Steve protests.

Barbara takes a deep breath, releases in a heavy sigh. "Maybe I panicked. But all I could think about was getting help, all I could think about was 'What am I going to do if he dies?'"

With that, her voice breaks.

"Now Barbara," Steve reaches a comforting hand to her shoulder. "I'm not going to die. I fell is all—"

"I know you're not going to die—now! But I didn't know that then!"

Steve and Barbara have been married for over fifty years. Like any of us, on thousands of occasions over the course of that time and without incident, Steve has wakened in the night, gotten out of bed, done his business, and returned to bed safely. Bathroom break: a non-event.

Until two weeks ago.

Now I'm in their home and we're discussing, or trying to discuss, what they most want to keep when they relocate to assisted living. It's a challenge to keep them on point, since the call for help still seems to be up for debate.

"Everyone is fine," David reassures them. "And we're going to make sure you stay 'fine'. That's why we're finding you a better place to live."

"Sure," Steve agrees, "nothing wrong with living in a better place. It's just that we know our way around here and everything's familiar. We know all our neighbors and they know us—"

"Safer place, Dad," David modifies. "I'm sure you'll like it, maybe it won't seem better at first, but eventually you'll get used to it and the thing is, it's safer. It's a safer place for you and Mom to live."

"Why? They don't have bathrooms?" Steve asks stubbornly.

"They have orderlies or assistants or whatever they call those strong, young men who work there. They can pick you up off the floor just as easy as you please." Barbara says. "Or are they RNs?"

"Well," Steve huffs. "I certainly don't plan on having to be picked up off the floor a second time!"

"You didn't plan to be on the floor this time, did you? But there you were and there was nothing I could do about it!" Barbara retorts.

"Maybe we could get you some barbells, nothing too heavy, just something to build up those muscles a bit instead of jumping ship—"

"Dad, it's not just the fall and you know it. You and Mom are in your eighties—your health is starting to decline and Darla and I worry about you—"

"I still think somebody moved my slippers—"

"And who would move your slippers? Who lives here with you besides me? Are you saying you think I moved your slippers, is that what you're saying?"

Steve shakes his head, purses his lips, as if contemplating the mystery of it. "I don't know who could have done it. But if I'd known they were moved, I would have walked around them."

"Don't be ridiculous! Why would I move your slippers?"

"Mom. Dad. Forget the slippers, okay? This woman is here to help you move to a safer place to live and you need to give her your attention and decide what you're taking with you. Please, can we just get on with it?"

Steve looks at me and shrugs. Barbara steps into the kitchen and says, "I can't imagine not packing up pretty much everything in here—I use it all at least occasionally."

David clearly loves his parents and seems genuinely concerned for their well-being and safety. He describes receiving the middle-of-the-night phone call from the hospital and the unexpected panic attack he experienced.

"I thought I was having a heart attack!" he says. "Losing your cool must be a genetic thing I get from my parents. My wife Darla was the only one who stayed calm. I don't know what I would have done without her."

He had the thirty minute drive to the hospital to collect himself, but when he arrived, David found his mother nearly hysterical. He tried to calm her, but ultimately she was given a sedative and joined her husband in recovery!

"Mom and Dad are both still so healthy, I guess I just wasn't ready to think about them getting hurt," he said to me on the phone when making the appointment.

"My wife and kids are only a few minutes away from the place we found and so I'm hoping it will work out better for all of us—they'll get to see their grandkids more often and we can get there in a hurry if we're needed . . . I mean, what am I supposed to do, wait until something really terrible happens to one of them before I do anything?"

I'm explaining to Barbara the space restrictions of the one-bedroom apartment they're moving into and which I've previewed before arriving. The more I outline the reduction of space, the more Barbara grows perplexed, as if I'm not understanding something.

"But what about when our friends come over? The Johnsons from across the street almost always visit us on Sundays for dessert and coffee. They bring their two girls and Roxie, their sweet little bichon, and I serve pie or a something I've baked special. I have to have my cake tins, and pie plates—and my spring-form pan for my grandmother's cheesecake recipe."

"When your friends want to visit, you can always make special arrangements with the dining room, they may even have a late afternoon dessert tray," I respond, wondering how much chance David has had to hash out the details of the assisted living lifestyle with his parents. "As far as the contents of the house, we can take as much of what is important to you as possible. But since there is less space there than there is here, you're going to have to make choices and compromises—quite a lot of this is going to have to be left behind or given away," I explain further.

I can see a wave of emotions cross her face: A little more than two weeks ago, Barbara had none of the concerns I'm presenting today.

"Left behind? Given away? But I use these things," she persists.

"Everything in the house has to be evaluated in terms of your priorities," I answer. "You won't be able to take everything, so we have to decide what is more important than something else."

Barbara looks at Steve for interpretation. "It's not like we're hoarders. There's very little in the house we don't use or need," she says.

"So the new place is smaller," Steve answers. "Not much we can do about it now, Barbara." He picks up the salt and pepper shakers from the counter. "I suppose we could do without these. . . ."

"Think about it, Mom," David volunteers, catching the end of our conversation as he enters the room from checking in by phone with his wife. "You don't have to cook anymore, except maybe for special occasions at our house. The new place is going to prepare meals for you, remember? It's like being on permanent vacation."

"I don't want to be on vacation. When I'm home, I want to be home. Is there anything wrong with that?"

"Nothing wrong with it, Mom," David says. "It's just that you're not going to need most of this kitchen stuff because you won't be cooking your own meals."

"I like cooking the meals," Barbara answers.

"I know you do, Mom, but you've been doing it for over fifty years—how good is it that you're going to be able to take a break?" and he chuckles and attempts an affectionate hug. She wriggles out of it uncooperatively.

"Nobody makes meat loaf like your mom," Steve says wistfully.

"You can come to our house and cook the meat loaf," David answers. "And probably the new place will make something better that maybe Mom doesn't make so well—"

"Name one thing," Barbara demands.

Steve takes a shot at it: "Well, there is your tuna casserole— I've been telling you for a while now that casserole doesn't take like it used to, you forgot an ingredient or something. It used to be pretty good, but the last ten years or so—"

"There is no missing ingredient," Barbara snaps. "Your taste buds are off. I told you to ask the doctor about it. . . ."

"See there? I'm sure the new place makes a great tuna casserole," David says, "and I'm sure you'll both love it."

Steve and Barbara stare at their son as if he is speaking Chinese.

In the garage, Steve is taken aback to discover David doesn't want his tools.

"I have tools, Dad," David says.

"Well I know you have tools, but you don't have my tools," Steve clarifies.

David looks helplessly at Barbara and me. "Right. But I do have tools. . . ."

"Son, I can't be using your tools when I'm used to my own. I don't want to try to figure out your stuff with all those bells and whistles, I just want to use what I know how to use already— "

"Use it when, Dad? What are you talking about?"

"For when I want to fix stuff."

"What stuff?" Barbara asks. "When was the last time you fixed anything, Steven? I've been complaining about that front door since last winter—"

"Now that was just because I haven't been able to find the right tool," Steve says. "And it's beside the point. The point is: just because I'm moving into some new place doesn't mean I'm not going to need to fix a thing or two now and then. And when I do, I want to use my tools, not his."

He turns to me, waving his arms around to include everything. "Figure on the whole kit and caboodle going to my son's house. I'll sort through it when I'm there puttering—"

"Puttering? What puttering?" David asks.

"Honestly, Steven. You haven't puttered since forever—"

"A man putters. He doesn't throw out the tools he's been collecting all his life just because maybe he's been taking a break from it for a while."

"And how is that different from my macramé yarns? They got voted out without as much as a conversation—"

"This is not some fly-by-night hobby I tried once or twice, Barbara. This is a man's tools. All of a sudden we're picking up and moving to some strange place that forces me to do my puttering in my son's garage and I don't think it's too much to ask—"

"Okay, Dad," David concedes, nervously registering his father's rising tone. "It's okay, I can take the tools. We'll send them to the house and work it out later. You can putter in our garage when the mood takes you."

"That's all I ask," Steve answers. "A man needs what he needs."

"And a wom—" Barbara starts to jump in, changes her mind. Instead she says, "Do we have time for some nice homemade lemon pie and coffee before we do the bedroom?"

We take a much needed break and but not necessarily a restful one: it seems like no matter how the conversation starts, it seems to end up rehashing the night of Steve's fall.

"I bet you could look it up on your internet just how many times someone falls and dies," she is saying to David as we enter the "crime" scene.

"Watch where you step," she advises me over her shoulder and pointing to dark stains in the carpet. "I haven't had time to work on getting all that blood out. David says it's not really necessary since we're leaving.

"Especially at our age," she continues about the internet. "I probably saved your father's life by dialing for help!"

"Mom, I'm not arguing with you. I'm glad you made the call—"

"I just needed a minute—God knows I would have tried harder if I'd known it was going to come to this."

"Well, I wish you had tried a little harder, I wish I had tried a little harder—"

"I just tripped over my slippers—what's the big deal?"

And there it was, the bewildering truth at the core of it all: he just tripped. It's something that could happen to any of us, yet for most of us, life altering consequences won't happen as a result. But that singular event set into motion an entire restructuring of Steve's life—and Barbara's! He just tripped—and that changed everything that was familiar to them about their lives. He just tripped—and nothing from that moment on would be the same. He just tripped—and now he and Barbara were on a course that would take them out of the house they have lived in for fifty years, the home and memories they had created together, the comfort zone of their friends and the familiar—abruptly taken away without any advance notice or preparation.

David had responded quickly, spurred by his own reaction to his father's fall and motivated by genuine, loving concern for his parents. He didn't want to wait until something more serious happened. He was being prudent and proactive.

And in my experience, the longer he waited to take action after the incident, the more likely Steve and Barbara would have found reasons to postpone doing anything so drastic and the more susceptible David may have been to their resistance.

I don't personally know what conversations took place between them about the move or about the community into which they were moving. It's very possible David's parents turned a deaf, resistant ear to what he was telling them. Or, maybe in all the rush of doing what needed to be done, David failed to effectively integrate them in the process. Maybe when they toured their new home, his parents were in such denial that they just couldn't fully take in the implications of it as their new residence.

What I do know is that emotionally, Steve and Barbara had not resolved the incident that had so dramatically altered their lives. Two weeks had not been long enough for them to process the impact Steve's fall was having on where and how they lived. It was clear to an "outsider" like me, that Barbara was struggling with guilt and second-guessing her decisions from that night. And Steve was utterly bewildered how something so ordinary as tripping in his own home had turned their lives inside-out.

Just as David had not really thought about his parents getting hurt, clearly his parents weren't prepared for it either. They hadn't reconciled that at their age, and despite good health, one unfortunate event could initiate a series of events that would forever change their lives.

"I just tripped over my slippers—what's the big deal?" reminds us that timing is specifically unique to every situation; that decisions affecting permanent changes in residence have to be laced with a compassionate understanding of the multiple layers they impact; and that we need to stay sensitive to the "process" when major life changes occur. Acts of love must bear the hallmark of benevolent timing!

Patience is power. Patience is not an absence of action; rather it is "timing". It waits on the right time to act, for the right principles and in the right way.

— Fulton J. Sheen

CHAPTER SEVEN

"Everything appeared to be fine—when did these changes happen and why didn't we notice?"

"She said she didn't want to call and bother me," Patty says balancing a two-year old precariously on her hip while she tries to unlock the apartment door. She's a young thirty-something, brunette, brown eyes, cherub face, short and probably petite under normal circumstances. But right now she's really as wide as she is tall.

"Can I help you with that?" I ask.

"I think I got it." Patty shifts her very pregnant belly for slightly easier access to the lock, grunts audibly as she stretches to reach with the key, and succeeds in swinging the door open. "So instead of waiting for me to help, Mom tries to pull out the Christmas decorations in the closet using the kitchen chair, of all things, and I say, 'Mom, why didn't you get the ladder?'

"And she says 'What ladder? The ladder you're talking about disappeared when we sold the house five years ago.'

"And I say, 'Even still, you know standing on a chair isn't safe.'

"And she says, 'Honey, that's all there was.'

"And I say 'See? Just another reason you should have waited.'"

Patty immediately plops into the first chair inside the apartment and unloads her daughter on the carpet to play with some squeaky toys she pulls from her diaper bag. "And sure enough she falls and breaks her hip and her wrist. You wouldn't think with the floor being carpeted but something in the way she fell or how she landed—who knows? She had to crawl to the phone to dial for help. Can you imagine how painful that must have been? I mean she's only sixty, who would have thought? Then when they were treating her, the doctors noticed something not quite right with how she was answering their questions. So they ran some additional tests and diagnosed early signs of dementia. Dementia! At sixty! So with that and the diabetes on top of the physical recovery from the breaks, they've recommended assisted living."

She drags her free hand through her hair. "The strange thing is I talk to my mom on the phone at least three times a week. It's not like I've really been worried about her, but I know she gets lonely. And I haven't noticed anything! She's coherent and just as active as she's always been—eats out with her girlfriends, goes shopping at the mall, attends church on Sunday, watches "Dancing with the Stars" every week. As far as I can tell she's as normal as I am!

Her doctor says the dementia could have been accelerated by the fall, but that it's likely she's had it for a while. So I keep replaying our conversations trying to figure out what I missed! Since the accident, it's pretty easy to notice the little gaps in logic when Mom is talking, like some of the pieces of what she's saying don't quite connect. But before? You'd think her own daughter would notice dementia if anybody would, but I was clueless!"

The apartment is small and more cluttered and unkempt than most. The floors are strewn with piles of newspapers and magazines, empty half-folded, paper grocery bags and discarded plastic bags. There's an ironing board set up in one corner of the living room with three overflowing clothes baskets sitting next to it.

But most predominantly are dozens upon dozens of houseplants. They crowd every available space. Yet, not a single one of them is thriving and most look like they've lost the battle to survive.

"Mom fancies herself as having a green thumb," Patty observes, taking in the room with me. "Like that wasn't a sure sign of dementia—duh!"

I'm there primarily because Patty is just too pregnant to handle the work of the move herself. But I also suspect she's hiring a little moral support.

"This place looks like an alien has invaded! Mom was never a neat freak, but we were raised in a clean home and taught to put things away and pick up after ourselves. I walk in and my first reaction is 'Who lives here?'"

On the couch are three trays stacked on top of one another, each containing soiled dishes from a meal eaten in front of the television. I spot orange prescription bottles in every room—some missing lids and tipped over with pills spilling out, many empty and discarded. Bags of snack foods, in various stages of consumption, decorate the couch and loveseat like pillows.

"Seeing the house like this just made me sick. I feel so responsible—like I've been neglecting her. But with this one still in diapers and another on the way, it's just been easier for Mom to come to our house or meet halfway at the I-Hop for breakfast. It's been months since I came to the house. The doc says probably most of this mess is symptomatic of the dementia, and if I'd been here, I would have picked up on it. But it just never occurred to me to be concerned about how Mom was living. She's only sixty!"

With great effort, Patty collects her little one and follows me into the kitchen, where she collapses again at the table. Her daughter fidgets a minute, and then surrenders to sleep.

Patty laughs, stroking her daughter's hair lightly. "What I wouldn't give to join her!"

I continue my visual inventory of items that will require packing. We make a decision to take the table and agree on four chairs instead of six.

"I'll need help transferring the contents of the refrigerator and freezer to our house. They're both full. I find out now, after-the-fact, that Mom's lost all interest in putting together a meal. So she's been living on take-out, delivery and microwave dinners. And I ask myself, 'Is that dementia, or is that just a woman living alone?'"

Ultimately, once the trash is removed and the plants are put out of their misery, there isn't a lot to sort through and the move progresses easily. My team packs everything in one short weekend to meet the deadline for her mother's transfer from rehab to assisted living on Monday.

"Thanks for listening to me go on and on about my mom," Patty says by phone when I call to say the move is complete. "My husband Allen is sick of hearing about it, but the truth is I feel so guilty. I feel like I wasn't paying enough attention or that someone's waiting around the corner to charge me with criminal negligence!"

She laughs. "Allen says it's just hormones making me obsess over no big thing and that once I have the baby, it'll go away. We can only hope, right?"

When I follow up a two weeks later to confirm everything went to her satisfaction, the conversation is brief. In the foreground is the shrill cry of an infant.

"I had the baby two days after we checked Mom into assisted living," Patty informs me. "And maybe it's still too soon, but so far Allen was dead wrong: I don't feel any better about the whole thing with my mom. Hormones or not, I'm always going to wonder if somehow I failed her!"

"Oh my God!" Patty announces when I answer my cell phone eighteen months later. "It's deja vu all over again!"

This time she is calling about her grandmother.

Patty paints the picture of a life more demanding than ever: Allen has taken a better paying job but one that requires weekly overnight travel. In addition to raising the girls without his help during the week, she is still working full-time—and is five months pregnant with their third child!

"Every Wednesday I take my mom to dinner to spend a few hours with her," she tells me. "Allen calls it my penance, but it's not that so much. I just want to stay on top of how she's doing."

Her commitment to family extends to her grandmother, who lives fifty miles north. They talk regularly by phone but every six weeks or so she and her husband load up the kids on a Sunday afternoon for a road trip to Grannie's.

"My life couldn't be any more hectic, but I haven't forgotten what happened with my mom. So no matter how busy we are, I make sure we visit in person!" Patty says.

The story she proceeds to disclose is not uncommon to my experiences:

"When we visit, we only stay a few hours. The kids can be kind of hard on Grannie's nerves but she enjoys them in short bursts! Usually we bring food so she doesn't have to cook. Grannie's eighty-three and in great health, not like Mom, but we just want to make sure she's okay and give her a chance to see her grandkids.

"So yesterday we arrived with a bucket of chicken and side dishes and we're sitting at the kitchen table having a kind of picnic. Grannie seems as spry as ever and is laughing with the girls, but we can't help but notice how hungry she is!

I swear we sat there and watched her chow down six pieces of chicken all by herself!

"At first I just laughed and made a few jokes about Grannie and the Colonel, but there was something just not right about it. Allen and I look at each other and we're like, 'really?' and so I ask when the last time she ate was. She waves the question off with something about opening a can of soup for breakfast and that's when the alarms start to go off. I get up and go to the refrigerator and it looks like there's plenty of food in it. But when I start opening the Tupperware containers, I discover leftovers that look like science experiments! The milk is spoiled, and even the ketchup and mustard are way beyond expiration. There are a few vegetables still edible, but you can't find them for all the spoiled ones.

"You know that optical illusion, the young woman or the old witch? Well that's what it was like. Instead of seeing Grannie and the house in my usual way, all of a sudden I'm looking at the same thing and seeing it differently. Grannie is still Grannie, but now I catch the stains on the sleeve of her blouse and how wrinkled her skirt is. I notice both her shoelaces are in knots and the heels of her tennis shoes are rolled over from forcing her feet in and out.

"Then I realize how neglected the house looks—not cluttered or messy, but that the furniture has layers of dust and the floors need to be mopped. There's a huge stack of half-opened mail taking up most of one counter and the grocery list next to the phone only has two things written on it.

"So I grab Allen and we walk around the house and take inventory, I mean really take notice! And we find a dozen little things—no one thing by itself is damning so much as they are in total, you know? Like, the plants are alive, but really neglected. She actually does have a green thumb, the only one in the family, but you wouldn't know it to look at the plants that day. And the laundry is folded but laid out in piles upon piles that need to be put away. The clothes inside the dryer are damp and smell like they've been sitting in there for days. The bathroom faucet won't turn off and there's a steady trickle of water coming out. The shower curtain is moldy. Outside, the city trash containers are overflowing and flies are swarming everywhere.

"It's hard to explain because nothing was in-your-face wrong, but everything was just neglected, including Grannie. She's drives and she's been managing her life so well, especially for her age, but all of a sudden it was clear to us that she was losing it. Maybe Grannie noticed too and just didn't mention it; her generation isn't about to complain, they just make do. Or maybe she hadn't noticed either! How do you tell when you're not alert when you need to be alert to notice you aren't?

"Anyway, we had just visited six weeks before, so we had to ask ourselves: How long has it been like this? Since Grannie hadn't said anything, and because we weren't spending that much time there at any one visit, and because we were distracted with the kids and preoccupied with our own lives, we just hadn't picked up the signs.

"But how could we have not noticed the smell? Grannie always keeps fresh flowers around the house and uses different floral diffusers in every room. Usually her house smells like a flower garden! Now it smells like...old people!

"I thought I'd learned my lesson about being more directly involved after the fiasco with my mom, but Allen and I were involved, we had been visiting Grannie. And it still caught us by surprise.

"*Everything appeared to be fine—when did these changes happen and why didn't we notice?"*

We moved Patty's grandmother to an assisted living community only a few miles away from the one where her mother was residing. It went well, but despite my assurances otherwise, through it all Patty insisted on maligning herself as a "repeat offender" of "criminal neglect"!

The practical reality is that we are all creatures of habit and lulled by routine. We are all blinded by our expectation that things are the way they seem; we don't typically look beneath the surface.

It's not uncommon for even the most attentive of children to experience such a moment of reckoning with their parents. It can be provoked by catastrophe like the one Patty experienced with her mom. Or, like the optical illusion she described, some mundane event can cause us to inexplicably view the same thing from a new perspective.

There's no infallible way to protect against this except to understand that it happens. Adult children can set an intention to be more deliberate and observant in conversations and visits with parents. They might run through a mental checklist of things to notice when they are in a parent's home. They can ask, "What can I do for you?" and be probative about the response—parental needs can reflect changes in function and capability.

Aging parents may not recognize their own physical or mental decline and so the greater responsibility often rests on their children and loved ones. Regardless of good intentions and loving hearts, children can be distracted with their own lives or just miss the subtle signs that indicate the need for some kind of intervention. *"Everything appeared to be fine— when did these changes happen and why didn't we notice?"* is a call to be compassionate toward yourself, while engaging in a practice of more mindful visits and conversations with those we love.

There are things known and there are things unknown, and in between are the doors of perception.

—Aldous Huxley

CHAPTER EIGHT

*"She's just like her father—
except I could divorce him!"*

"Take them both if you want, Mother. It's yours to decide," Janice says somewhat primly.

"I have no trouble making a decision," Gloria says, studying two sweaters from the coat closet, one much heavier than the other. "I just asked if you knew whether the rooms have individual thermostats."

"I said I believe they do," Janice answers and when Gloria scowls, she adds, "You can call for yourself if you don't trust my answer."

"Like I don't have anything better to do," Gloria answers and tosses both sweaters into the packing box. "Better take them both. I'll be the one freezing to death and not be able to do a thing about it."

Janice stares at her mom for a moment, then says, "If you have any other questions, I'll be in the kitchen," and leaves the room.

Gloria looks at me, smiles gallantly and says, "What's next?"

Gloria is a retired school teacher, now in her late seventies. She's attractive, tall and slim and in remarkably good shape. Her townhouse is on a golf course where she plays three times a week. On the other four days, she puts in ten miles on a stationary bike we've already labeled to be moved.

She dresses conservatively in pressed trousers and stylish blouses and has her white hair cut in a fashionable bob. On the middle finger of her left hand she wears a turquoise stone ring, a treasure she picked up in Santa Fe, New Mexico after a generous divorce settlement thirty-some years ago.

After Gloria retired from teaching, she traveled extensively with a senior's tour group and developed a network of friends who encouraged her to pursue artistic interests she expressed during trips. While on a Caribbean cruise, Gloria became fascinated with the creative possibilities of sea shells and decided to pursue them as her artistic medium. This developed into a small business of frames, mirrors, and other household items decorated with sea shells she collected on her own travels. The second bedroom is set up as a studio where she arranges just the right combination of shells and glues them to items to transform them into knickknacks and collectibles she can sell on the internet or craft shows.

The business has become less active in recent years and the studio will be dismantled with the move. But a few of her signature creations will be making the trip—in particular, an elegantly shelled, picture-window sized mirror hanging in the dining room that requires special handling. Gloria is a little anxious about it—but not nearly as much as I am.

I've already scoured the internet for matching replacement shells, just in case.

Janice, her daughter, is shorter, darker and heavier than her mother. Also attractive, also dressed conservatively. She lives with her husband and two young children in West New York, New Jersey. Her sister, the other daughter, lives in California so Janice has taken a week off from work and her family to oversee the move. She isn't quite in drill sergeant mode, but she's keeping a close eye on the clock and is driving our schedule in a restrained and resolute manner. Her overseer's role is frequently interrupted by phone calls from her husband and kids, who seem to have questions that only she can answer. She steps out of the room to handle the calls privately, but I can see her frustration mount at juggling two roles.

Janice is the one who contacted me on behalf of the family. She explained that while her mother is in excellent physical shape, Janice had noticed memory lapses and behavior changes in recent months. Gloria had summarily rejected her concern. But when Gloria began turning in golf scores on par with Tiger Woods, her golfing buddies contacted Janice to express concern that her outstanding scores were an offense of memory rather than integrity.

With this, Gloria was forced by her own peers to face the problem and agreed to tests that then diagnosed the dementia. To cushion the transition into assisted living, Janice scoured the area for just the right place for her mother—a community with a golf course-like setting on 1000 acres—and made arrangements for the move.

Gloria's home is beautiful: It has a one-level, open area floor plan with a screened-in patio facing a lush green fairway and sculptured pond. She has converted the patio into a solarium bird sanctuary, overflowing with plants, trees, vines and song birds in ornate cages. In the entry is an eight foot tall Grandfather's clock, whose chime resounds throughout the house most of the time we're there. Each time the hour strikes, I see Janice glance at her watch, as if confirming yet another hour has passed.

The great room has a large stone fireplace with windows on either side. On the mantle there are four of Gloria's 28-piece collection of ceramic roosters. Others are tastefully positioned throughout the house and encased in cabinets and a breakfront piece in the dining room opposite the shelled mirror.

It is not easy for Gloria to narrow her collection to five that will accompany her to her new home.

"Which one?" Janice asks suspending two up in the air by the neck, one in each hand.

"Oh, I guess the one on the right," Gloria answers hesitantly.

"Which one?" Janice asks again, holding the next two up by the neck, and so on, whittling the collection down by comparison.

"Wait!" Gloria protests. "I changed my mind. I like this one more than the other one you held up, but I don't like it as much as the one I said I didn't like in that pair you held up before."

Janice tries to comply. "You mean this pair?" she asks, pointing to two on her right. "Or this pair?" she says, pointing to another set on her left.

"Neither of them. I'm talking about that pair at your feet."

Janice looks down, starts to pick up two but Gloria waves her to another pair on the floor behind them.

"Those, I like both of those," Gloria clarifies.

"Mother, you like them all, but we agreed you can only take five."

"I know what we agreed. I'm just saying I like those two in particular."

"Okay, so let's pack them."

"Not just yet, I haven't decided on the others and I might change my mind."

"We've been through the others. You just said you liked these two 'in particular'."

"'In particular' is not final, I'm still deciding. Just put them down and I'll figure it out myself. Don't they need you in the other room?" Gloria asks hopefully.

Janice exhales, places the roosters carefully onto the coffee table, glances noticeably at her watch, and leaves.

"I'm late, I'm late, for a very important date," Gloria sing-songs under her breath as she then matter-of-factly chooses five roosters from the brood surrounding us and hands them to me.

"I'm going to miss those roosters," Gloria says of the ones headed for Goodwill. "It took me a lot of years to collect them."

"I'm sure their next owners will treasure them also," I say.

"It's not the same, though, is it?" Gloria says and walks away.

The bedroom is magnificent with cathedral ceilings, a fireplace and another patio containing a flowing water sculpture made of stones, rocks and, of course, sea shells. The walk-in closet is as large as most bedrooms and Gloria's clothes are neatly organized by season, color and kind. It's a wonder to behold.

"Lot of memories tied up in all my finery," Gloria says pulling out what looks like a Mexican poncho. "Cancun . . . my first scuba dive . . . tequila shooters and lots of dancing. I went with my friends Cynthia and Hilary . . . no, it was Cynthia and Greta. No, not Greta, her name was . . . she was a new friend of Cynthia's . . . or was it Hilary and Cindy? Cindy, Cynthia. . . ."

Gloria's voice trails off and she lapses into a few seconds of thoughtful silence.

"Well, at any rate, it was fun," she says at last. "And this can go," she adds, tossing the poncho onto the floor. "Don't think there will be much need for fun clothes where I'm headed."

Sorting through Gloria's wardrobe is tedious, time-consuming and exhausting. Occasionally an outfit reminds her of her travels or a man she dated or an event she attended and as Gloria reminisces nostalgically, the process takes on a somber air. We don't falter in our mission, and Gloria is reasonably quick with her decisions, but this is the fourth day of the overall process, and she's getting tired. As that happens, resentment toward the move becomes even more apparent.

"Oh, that dress is far too glamorous for what I'm destined for," she says waving away a moderate blue silk dress suit.

"If I can't take them all, then I'll just take whatever," she responds to a stack of neatly folded sweater tops. "Set aside something suitably bland and toss the rest."

When I pull out a drawer of scarves and gloves, Gloria says, "Just grab something warm and I'll make do."

Janice pokes her head in every so often but Gloria is quick to send her away. "We've got it handled, dear," she says coolly and Janice doesn't argue. She does, however, remind us of how long we've been at it.

"Going on four hours now," she says. "'Bout done?"

"You'll be the first to know, dear daughter," Gloria answers with a subtle but unmistakable edge.

The wardrobe takes longer than estimated; Gloria seems to have shoes, accessories and clothes for every season, every occasion, and every geographic location. Just when I think we've got it handled, we pull out a box or basket or hamper with yet another round of selections. I try to "lump" process some of the stuff, but Gloria is determined to sort through each item and I recognize she is re-experiencing the memories before she says goodbye. So we take as much time as she needs.

We expected the fifth day to be minimal, but there's still plenty to do. With exhaustion and the strain of the deadline, all the gloves are off between mother and daughter. Janice is issuing directions to my crew like General Patton and Gloria is readied to spring at the first person who says "good morning". I can only do so much to keep them out of each other's way since there is a limited number of areas left to be packed.

Around noon, Gloria and I are sitting on the settee in the solarium discussing the birds. She's made arrangements for a grocery list of friends in her townhouse community to assume their care: the yellow canary with the blemish on his beak goes to Jan; the purple finch with the lavender breast feathers goes to her neighbor's grandson Teddy, and so on. There are almost two dozen birds and we're only on number seven. Just when I think we're gaining on it, they take flight, confusing both of us, and we have to start over.

"I'd much rather that they all go to the same home so they can stay together," Gloria explains. "I wanted my grandsons to have them, but, of course, Janice refused to allow it. Not sure what the problem was, you'd have to ask my daughter—"

"Ask me what?" Janice asks entering the room and catching the tail end of the conversation.

I don't see this going anywhere good and try to divert the conversation to the pretty little white parakeet, but Gloria jumps in. "Why you won't let the boys take my precious song birds. I wanted all my little friends to go to the same home, but you're forcing me to split them up."

"I'm certainly not forcing you to do anything," Janice protests. "It just wouldn't work out for us to take them."

"Even though it would keep them together," Gloria persists.

"I would be the one who ended up taking care of them and you know it. The boys have too many other after-school activities in addition to their homework—"

"It's always about you, isn't it?" Gloria growls.

"It isn't about me; it's about making sure the birds are well cared for. I know the boys and I know they won't do it, so it would be left to me—"

"You, you, you! Everything is always about you," Gloria snaps. "Just once, I'd like to see you do one thing for me—"

"One thing?" Janice's voice is suddenly terse. With guarded precision, she asks, "Is that really what you just said, Mother? 'One thing?'"

"Yes, that's exactly what I said. You expect everyone to hop to your schedule, do what you—"

"Fine!" Janice interrupts. "Have it your way, let's make it all about me. . . ."

She leans down to get squarely in her mother's face and says with drawn out relish: "I don't want your noisy birds stinking up my home and robbing me of precious time! Satisfied?"

She whirls around but is not quite out of earshot when Gloria, as if speaking to me but clearly intended for her daughter's ears, delivers her coup de grâce: *"She's just like her father—except I could divorce him!"*

It's reasonable to assume that Gloria and Janice, not unlike many mothers and daughters, had decades of conflicts, disagreements, disappointments, hurts, wounds, and life between them that could have fueled an argument on that last day—and which had nothing at all to do with song birds.

Janice appeared to be a devoted daughter. I don't know the precise circumstances, but it was clear to me that Janice's family was not making it easy for her to be away from them. Their calls, the interruptions, and whatever demands then of her attention and energy were intruding on the task at hand and probably fueling frustration and guilt about having to be away. What I do know is that over the course of the process leading to Gloria's relocation, Janice had facilitated the medical assessments that diagnosed her mother, was resourceful in finding a community that had the same luxury resort feel as where her mother had been living, took a week from work that was anything but vacation, and then worked five, 12-hour days to make it happen on schedule and as budgeted.

Most of us would struggle to describe such behavior as selfish!

Dementia and Alzheimer's are complex and interrelated and stress fuels the symptoms of both. I know from experience that when people with dementia find themselves in circumstances that strain their abilities, resources and emotions, they are inclined to anger or tears, sometimes in sudden outbursts. Gloria was becoming increasingly symptomatic—with irritability, caustic comments and ultimately the very personal attack on her daughter. Yet I doubt neither mother nor daughter associated any of this with Gloria's diagnosis of dementia.

Janice had expressed to me that the two daughters anticipated that Gloria's family and loved ones would experience more of the "good" of her mother under more controlled circumstances. But it's highly unlikely that Gloria shared that hope. She was experiencing all the predictable emotions of losing her home, her friends, her lifestyle, her independence—in addition to dealing with progressive dementia and the behavioral reactions it can cause.

The harsh exchange I witnessed may have been the first time Gloria expressed that she saw Janice's father in her daughter, or maybe it was a shared understanding that Janice exhibited some or many of the traits, mannerisms and physical characteristics of her father. Perhaps Gloria had used that similarity against Janice on other occasions when she was angry; or, perhaps in the strain of the move, some intangible dislike between them was given shape and form for the first time.

It is also possible that it may not have been Janice herself, but the circumstances that fueled Gloria's anger against her daughter. The sheer strain of the move could have rekindled the emotional memories of her divorce and found a target in Janice simply because her daughter was there. Gloria's explosion could have had nothing at all to do with Janice resembling her father, nor her mother having a personal dislike for her daughter; it might have been directly related to the recreation of emotional duress she had endured years before.

It could have everything to do with dementia or nothing to do with dementia; it could have everything to do with family strife or nothing at all. But when dementia is a factor—and in various degrees and progressively as we age, it almost always is—the responsibility for managing situations falls more heavily on the adult children. Janice could have jumped into the fray any number of times, but repeatedly chose the less combative path. I have no doubt she heard her mother's accusation as she was leaving the room, but she kept walking.

"She's just like her father—except I could divorce him!" explores the evasiveness of truth when dementia is a factor. It invites us to recognize the complex factors at play, under any circumstances, when a parent is leaving their home, but especially when dementia is involved. In such situations, adult children are challenged to perceive beyond appearances and act with gentle understanding and sometimes, fierce constraint.

Appearance is something absolute,
but reality is not that way—
everything is interdependent, not absolute.

—Dalai Lama

Chapter Nine

"I can't live another day around all these old people!"

The two-bedroom townhouse could be the setting for a Shakespearean play. Lois, the mother, is center stage, clearly the only place she's comfortable being, and is resplendent in a boldly flowered lavender and mauve caftan, worn over red stretch pants and fashionable but worn, black leather boots. An inch of white shows at the roots of her Clairol dark brunette hair, most of which is tucked into a chunky knitted, slouchy beanie beret, stylishly tilted on her head—so much so it looks like it might just topple off. I want to just reach over and save it.

Though it's been years since she saw eighty, she'll still somewhat successfully managing to apply dark black fake lashes that facilitate a flirty eye-flutter that happens every time one of my male workers passes within proximity. Her lipstick is red, her eyelids blue and her cheeks bright pink. She has hammered copper jewelry that dangles off ear lobes, both wrists and her neck.

She speaks with her hands, long red acrylic nails darting through the air as she talks. She's relatively lithe for an old lady and moves with full body gestures anyone on stage would envy. Right now she's fluttering around the room in dramatic "woe-is-me" fashion reacting to the flurry of moving activity around her.

Enter stage left: Neil is the quintessential obedient son. In sharp contrast to his mother, he is just a regular guy: brown hair, brown eyes, average height and weight, blue jeans, denim shirt, scuffed work boots. He's in his mid-fifties, and occasionally pulls out wire-framed reading glasses to tend to some chore. He says very little and what he does is mostly to acknowledge some demand his mother has made. Even on the phone when he called to make arrangements for the move, he was soft-spoken and circumspect. He didn't elaborate on the reasons for moving his mother to assisted living except to say it had become medically imperative, but aside from possibly telling, frequent trips to the patio for a smoke, she seems mentally alert, spry and able.

The third in our cast of characters is Howard, the boyfriend. He has just arrived and Lois' batting eyelashes reflect her spirited interest in him. Howard, only a few years older than Neil, indulges her obvious affection—though never taking his keen eyes off the black leather couch, as yet unassigned. Lois would like to take it if there's room where she's moving, but Howard's living room has been converted into a pool room and the big couch would be just right for lounging between shots.

Today at least, Howard is attired as the Man in Black: jeans, t-shirt, pea coat, and topsiders. There's little contrast between the black of his irises and his pupils and his dark hair is dramatically slicked back into a ponytail. Adding to the somewhat sinister effect, he smiles with only one corner of his mouth, so it comes across as more of a sneer. Though it's clear he has a second agenda that involves material goods, he's not entirely unlikeable. He seems to satisfy the role of Lois's portable audience, following her around with smooth reassurances and undisputed agreement.

There's a "Howard" corner in the living room that expands with more and more items the longer he's in the house.

"I want you to have the bistro table," Lois insists. "And take the chairs. Can you use the patio table or is that too much?"

"You know I'll make room for whatever you want me to have," Howard assures her. "The bistro table would rock in the pool room, especially opposite the leather couch, if that happens. And the patio set would be perfect for wine at sunset—but you have to promise to come to my place and enjoy it with me."

"A loaf of bread, a jug of wine and thou," they launch together as if on cue and Lois giggles with delight.

Their moment is interrupted by the soft clang of a screw driver hitting metal. Neil looks up from the floor lamp he's repairing for his mother and gives an apologetic shrug. This is the third time he's had to fix it; Lois keeps knocking it over while practicing her dance routine—the one she imagines performing at the local community theater one day.

Howard looks over as if noticing Neil for the first time. He adds awkwardly, "Unless, of course, you want Neil and Dorothy to have the patio set."

"Don't be silly," Lois insists with a wave off into the air. "I'm sure they already have everything they need. I'd much rather you took both sets where I know they'll be appreciated."

Neil doesn't weigh in, just adjusts his reading glasses and carries on with the lamp.

"It's whatever you want," Howard answers, giving Lois's hand a comforting squeeze. "I just don't want you worrying about anything. Take what you need and just trust that everything else will find a good home."

"It's just so difficult to know what to take and what to leave behind," Lois laments. "Those people just live in a different world than the one I know. What am I ever going to find in common with them?"

She's talking about the people residing at the assisted living community she's moving into. She's made no bones about her dismay at being surrounded by "them".

"I'm still on the road to new adventures and experiences—I'm an artist, for heaven's sake! What will happen to me when every direction I look there are decrepit, old—"

Just then Ken, one of my workers subcontracted for special handling of a three-dimensional mirror, walks through the room in route to his truck for more packing materials. He's twenty-something, and buff.

"Oh, please tell me you aren't leaving yet!" Lois interrupts herself, stepping nimbly into his path. "I'm depending on you boys to brighten up this dreary day!" She throws in an eye flutter for emphasis.

"No, Ma'am," he answers a little self-consciously, embarrassed by their sixty year age difference. "I'm just making a run to the truck."

"Oh for heaven's sake, call me Lois. 'Ma'am' makes me feel old," she says with a dismissive flutter of her fingers. He nods cooperatively, moves around her and is nearly out the front door when Lois calls after him, "Don't be gone long!"

She turns her attention back to Howard as if just remembering. "Darling, you did take care of that little errand we talked about, didn't you?"

"Of course," he answers. "Your wish is my command."

"You take such good care of me," she beams and gives his cheek a pat. "How could I possibly manage without you?"

Neil tests the lamp, sees it's working and sets it aside to start on the repair of a footstool.

Lois and I finalize a few more selections, go back and forth on the couch and finally agree to take it. If it doesn't work, Howard will be there to direct my crew to his apartment. When I suggest we move to the bedroom to sort through her wardrobe, Lois agrees but issues a directive to Neil before she leaves the room: "Son, make sure to replace all my batteries with new ones, check the alarm clock, my remotes, and the emergency flashlights. Run to the store if you need to."

"I was going to go ahead and start loading up my stuff," Howard interjects. "I know Neil is keeping busy around here, but I was hoping he could help me."

"Of course, he can help you!" Lois answers quickly. "Silly me for not offering! That's what he's here for, no reason he can't do both!"

It's all she needs to say. Neil is up and has an armful of bistro table before Howard has had a chance to pull out his car keys.

The process of choosing clothes to make the move is, of course, a dramatic one. Every outfit is a tug of war: Lois couldn't possibly part with the red party dress, or the bling slippers or the black negligee set. Less in words than in dramatic affect, she makes it clear that life as she knows it would cease without every single one of her dozen cloaks and capes.

I doggedly talk her down to five, but am exhausted by her tenacity and insistence. The whole wardrobe-sorting process easily takes twice the time it should.

Curiously, despite wanting to take everything, Lois finds very little in her wardrobe that seems to suit the activities and lifestyle she imagines being forced to adopt at the assisted living community. "I can't think what they do with their day," she says rolling her eyes, her hand briefly touching her temple as if the very effort was giving her a migraine.

"I have a feeling that with this crowd, I could just throw on the same thing every single day and no one would even notice," she says, handing me two blouses to pack, one neon orange, the other chartreuse. "I wonder if they lose their ability to see color the same way we do?" she asks with genuine intrigue.

By "we", I figure out she's asking about everyone under 60—and her; and "they" is everybody living at the new community—except her.

"Of course, the biggest change for me," she says bringing both hands to rest on her breaking heart, "will be losing my studio. Neil insists on reminding me that I haven't used the potter's wheel in years but he's never really understood the artist that I am. One day I'll be moved to sculpt and will be utterly lost without all my tools!"

We are donating three hundred pounds of potting clay to one of the local art schools and I am thrilled they have agreed to pick it up and load it themselves, rather than us having to carry it up from the basement.

Adding to the schedule delay, Lois repeatedly calls for a nicotine break; on one occasion, she's gone far longer than usual and just when I start to notice how delightfully peaceful and quiet it is, she comes breezing in like Tinker Bell. "Those boys are just adorable, aren't they? I insisted they take a break and had to practically drag them away from their work. I told them they deserved a little refreshment—"

She gets my full attention at the mention of snacks and mistakes this for disapproval, quickly adding, "Just a bit of my special recipe, this yummy blend of lemonade, cranberry juice and green tea. I just love making up recipes, don't you? I insisted so don't you be giving those boys any grief. Goodness, what a pleasure it's been to have their help!"

My mouth waters thinking that I would have enjoyed a glass myself, though I suspect it's not personal. No doubt about it: Being male would have bolstered my position.

Lois and I keep plugging away at the bedroom and by the time we finish and return to the living room, Howard is long gone.

"He wanted to make the trip to unload now, just in case he needs to make a second run," Neil explains. "Depending on how many people he can find to help him, he'll meet us back here or at the community."

"The poor boy has to unload all by himself?" Lois laments. "Couldn't you have gone with him, Neil? It's not like we can't spare you here."

"Can't be two places at once," he answers, "and I thought it might be better if I stuck around here in case you needed an extra hand. . . ."

"That's fine, dear. But give him a call, won't you? Just to make sure he has help on the other end. I'd just hate for him to hurt his back or something from the exertion."

But when he calls, Neil finds out Howard is already done unloading and is having a beer on the patio, testing out his new furniture. "Have a plan, work a plan," we hear him say on speaker-phone, placed there so that 'we can all enjoy him', Lois's words. "Picked up a case of Bud on the way home and guys came out of the woodwork to help me. I didn't have to lift a finger."

"He's such a clever problem solver, isn't he?" Lois marvels to her son after the call.

"He sure is, Mom. A very resourceful guy," he answers and continues carrying hand-wrapped valuables that Lois insists he take in his own car to assure their safe transport and her peace of mind.

Because the mirror boys were delayed by tea and the wardrobe sorting so prolonged, our move-in timing is just enough off kilter to make the gathering at Lois's new one bedroom apartment an elbow-to-elbow traffic jam. With Howard, Neil, Lois, my three-man moving team, the two mirror specialists and me all vying for space, even the slightest move intrudes on someone else. Lois immediately dashes off to show the buff boys where to begin hanging the mirror, already taking delight in squeezing around them in the tight quarters.

Neil hesitates in the entry doorframe, seems to assess the hubbub, and then looks at me with a weary smile. He deliberately wipes his hands on the sides of his jeans, reaches into his wallet, removes a check and extends it to me. I take it and then look at him questioningly. He whirls a pointed finger around in a little tornado and says, "I trust you to make it right. Thanks for everything!"

Then he departs, Lois none the wiser.

"You're the wind beneath my wings. . . ." Lois is saying affectionately from the bedroom where she's taken Howard to give him the "tour". I maneuver around my crew to step into the room and immediately stop short: Howard and Lois are standing in front of the closet—but not the empty closet I'm expecting to fill with the wardrobe boxes waiting in the truck. Instead, the closet is miraculously already half full of clothes.

"Are those clothes?" I ask diplomatically, thinking about the afternoon we've spent whittling her wardrobe down to what I know from experience will fit into a ten-foot closet.

"Isn't my Howard just the greatest?" Lois exclaims proudly. "Look what he brought me!"

"You said it was life and death," Howard answers. "I just took the list you gave me and had two guys from shipping and receiving at work slip over here during lunch to bring them over—"

"You're my hero." Lois does the eye flutter thing again, playing to him and the audience that seems to never veer far from her imagination.

With this little contrived surprise, I know instinctively that I have hours of costume Armageddon to hash out with Lois.

But true to Neil's entrustment, we sort it all out and make it right.

Six months later I receive a call from Lois.

"Darling, you have to help move me out of here. I've already talked to Neil and found an apartment and he says I should deal with you directly. Do you think those two young men who moved my mirror could be available to help again? Can we do it immediately?"

We're on the phone, but I can visualize her tossing a feather boa over her shoulder, Hollywood sunglasses perched on her nose, red lips pursed in a tight little pout when she says, *"I can't live another day around all these old people!"*

The difference between Lois and most people who become residents of assisted living is that remarkably, Lois was given the option to leave. In my experience, this is practically unheard of. More often, it is as Lady Macbeth would have it: "What's done is done and cannot be undone."

I credit Neil with this. It would have been far easier and more convenient to insist that Lois simply live with it, regardless of her reasons for discontent. It's not unlike sending a child away to summer camp—they call home because they're lonely and scared and uncertain, but as parents, we assure them it's for their own good!

To the newly transplanted assisted living resident: You miss your own home? It hurts to say it and I'm sorry, but it's for your own good.

You hate everyone else controlling when to eat and what you can do? I'm sorry, but it's for your own good.

You think the people around you are dull, lifeless and old? I'm sorry, but it's for the best.

The decision to move Lois to assisted living was a "medical imperative", and could reasonably be construed as one of life and death and still, Lois was given the option to leave!

How remarkable is that?

Lois may have been unhappy over the loss of her home or the loss of freedom and control over her schedule, or may not have liked the limitations it placed on her love affair with Howard. But I have no doubt that the single-most compelling reason Lois wanted to leave was one of identity: she was an artist and even in her eighties, she was still elaborately interpreting her daily life experience with drama and gusto and she simply refused any stage that did not support that.

She refused to compromise and Neil had her back.

The heroine of this story was certainly Lois, big and bold and unapologetic, insisting to the very end that she stand true to herself without compromise.

But the real hero was Neil—the unremarkable son who showed himself to be exceptionally uncommon in the freedom he gave his mother to live her life as she chose.

We moved Lois to another apartment in a community where she could be surrounded by her "own people", a small artist's complex geared toward residents twenty and thirty years younger and without medical care, but replete with art, dance and acting classes and studios.

Lois spent her last few months in the full throes of artistic expression!

When I recall Lois's words, *"I can't live another day around all these old people!"* I think of Neil and associate the Serenity Prayer: *"God grant me the serenity to accept the things I cannot change, the courage to change the things I can, and the wisdom to know the difference."*

Lois was a mother who demanded center stage and insisted on a world that revolved around her and Neil made no attempt to change that. I'm equally certain any attempt to do so would have been impossible and would have only created chasms of conflict between them.

I don't know what Neil was like away from her world, but he seemed to have made peace with filling a role in her life that didn't compete with the one Lois needed for herself—a role that must have required he surrender his ego, his own agenda, perhaps even his own needs. He wasn't a man who cowered to her every need, but he was a son who served his mother and made no effort to correct or compromise the dramatic role she insisted on playing. I'm sure he must have had an opinion about the thirty year age difference between Howard and his mother, about the man himself or about the bistro table that got away. I'll never know what his true thoughts were because he so kindly and graciously allowed his mom to write, direct and star in her own dramatic expression of her life.

Unlike many of us as sons and daughters, parents, siblings, wives and husbands, Neil graciously accepted what he could not change.

When assisted living was more than Lois could bear, Neil could have relied on "it's for your own good", but instead, he had the courage to give Lois what she most wanted, the courage to allow her to reap the consequences, the courage to let her make her final transition perhaps earlier than she might have under medical care. He had the courage to change what he could to make her life better by her own standards, not his.

Aging adults want the most they can get out of the last years of their life and they often have strong opinions about how that needs to happen. These opinions may be compromised by mental deterioration or may just not be as compelling when weighed against other considerations. Children of aging adults want the same for their parents, but they often have also had to assume the role of making decisions on "behalf" of their parents, decisions that may override what the parent desires.

This process is always a delicate dance, but Neil and Lois played out theirs in a way that shines as an example of human spirit.

*The greatness of the man's power
is the measure of his surrender.*

—William Booth

Chapter Ten

"Do I have to do this anymore?"

"You sure you can you see okay?" I ask my mother. The movie previews have started and even though we're situated precisely in the middle row of the theater, half-way back from the screen, she seems to be squinting. No real surprise, given the last four years of radiation treatments for non-Hodgkin's tumors of the eye, but I want to make her as comfortable as possible. I live on the opposite coast as she so I have limited firsthand knowledge of what her vision limitations are and suspect her verbal renditions are greatly minimized. I'd really like to think she can make out the actors on the screen, and not just hear their voices.

"It's fine, not to worry," Nancy answers. "Let's just enjoy the movie."

Just like my mom. Always making the best of things. Over eight times we moved as a military family when I was growing up and every time she assured my three brothers and me that our new home, in a new city, with all new friends was going to be nothing but a terrific adventure.

And we believed her.

And it always was.

"Are you craning your neck?" I ask worriedly, sneaking a look at her while trying not to appear to be doing so.

"Don't be silly. Quit worrying and watch the movie, you're going to miss the important parts."

"Mom, the movie hasn't even started yet. You can't see at all, can you?"

"As well as can be expected. Now stop worrying," she assures me.

"'As well as can be expected'. That must mean you can't see the movie screen but you're okay with it because you came here not expecting to be able to see it?"

"I'm fine."

"We could move closer," I suggest, launching into problem solving, which is my way. Oldest child. Only daughter. Best friend.

"I'm fine," she insists again but I catch her closing one eye as if testing to see if using one eye produces better results than using two.

"Maybe eye drops would help." I start scrambling through my purse, knowing she knows that I know there aren't any.

It was a gamble at best, given her eye condition, but I'm in town for a week from New York and I wanted to get my mom out of the house; she's been spending far too much time at home since her husband, my stepfather, Tom died eight months ago in October, 2003.

"Fritzi, I can't see perfectly, but I can see just fine. Please relax and let's just watch the movie," she says and then, as if to reassure me, seems to open her eyes wider in a poorly executed, fake focus.

"Oh for heaven's sake," I mutter in a last ditch effort for success. "Try these." And I take the prescription glasses off my own nose and hand them to her. It's a gallant gesture, one born of absolute frustration, desperation, and guilt. If she can't enjoy the movie, there's no way I will either and the afternoon will be a complete bust.

She surprises me by not objecting and putting them on.

"Isn't that Goldie Hawn's daughter?" my mother asks peering at the screen. "She's cute, looks just like her mom."

"What? You can see her?" I ask in bewilderment.

My mother turns her head, my Sally Rafael, oversized glasses occupying two thirds of her small face, her eyes wide with amazement—and not the fake kind. "Fritzi!" she exclaims far too loud for the theater but neither of us cares. "I can see!"

The radiation treatment my mother underwent when she was first diagnosed with non-Hodgkin's disease immediately impaired her vision so severely that she was all but blind. A self-reliant woman used to doing and going, my mother would have none of it. A year into the treatment, she attended the San Diego Center for the Blind in Vista to learn ways to make the best of what seemed inevitable.

But in the second year and as her condition improved with the removal of a cataract, she gained much of her vision back, at least enough so to be able to resume many activities, particularly with her husband, my step-father, Tom's assistance. Those activities included returning to the Center for the Blind, but this time as an assistant cooking teacher.

"The poor woman can only see shadows," my mother explained, describing Kathy, the instructor of the class.

"Isn't that the point?" I ask.

"Well, there's no sense in my not helping out. It's the least I can do after all the help Kathy was to me."

My mother liked giving back; she valued the sense of purpose working at the Center gave to her life; she liked the adventure of taking on the challenge of the work and the sense of accomplishment it gave her to prevail over her weakened eyesight. She didn't like feeling vulnerable; refused to be a victim.

It was during those years that I first began thinking about ways to make living at home more viable for my mom, despite her physical frailties and handicaps. The phrase "Aging-in-Place" had not yet been coined; the practice of making adjustments to one's home to prevent the necessity of assisted living was not yet a popularly accepted one.

But I was my mom's advocate. We were best friends and had been since I arrived at birth to a woman who had just learned her husband Frederick had been killed in Korea. I was christened at my father's funeral, and though Nancy went on to remarry and bear three more children, she and I had a bond born from trauma that linked us in a way that is uncommon, even among those closest mother-daughter relationships.

Though my step-father offered to adopt me many times over the years to come, Nancy always refused. She insisted on honoring her first husband by keeping his name alive through me. In fact, although I was christened Priscilla Lee Muer, the name my father chose, everyone, including my mother, called me "Fritzi", going by the same German nickname as my father had.

When my mom suffered vision loss, I worried about her. I was in New York and living so far away filled me with guilt and anxiety. She and I talked every day by phone and later, when she became proficient with email, we developed a communication routine that helped reassure me of her well-being. Each morning she woke at 5:30 A.M., made a cup of instant coffee, ate half a banana, and met her friends at 6:15 for a two mile walk at a nearby park. Before she left the house, she would drop me a brief email saying good morning, so that if in New York, I had not heard from her by 10:00, I was on the phone checking on her.

My youngest brother died in 1998, but my other two brothers Tom and Jim lived locally with their own families and were devoted to Mom's care and well-being. Jim's work day with the local utility company ended at 3:30 P.M., so he made a habit of going to Mom's most days on the way home and tending the yard or helping her with odds and ends around the house.

My brother Tom was a lawyer in downtown San Diego, but on weekends he would visit Mom, bring groceries, take her to lunch or dinner and add his own touch to the yard and landscaping.

The practical reality was that they had always watched after Mom as diligently as I would if I were there. But I was not there. I lived in New York, was newly widowed, had a 19-year-old son, and owned and operated my own company called TransitionsUSA, which helped relocate aging adults to assisted living. I agonized over my mom's safety, particularly since her diagnosis of non-Hodgkin's, simply because I was not there in person and had to rely on others.

I had spent a lot of time thinking about ways to help my mom manage her vision loss. My background in engineering, environmental safety and senior living helped me single out problems and practical solutions. From afar, I started offering suggestions that I thought would help: additional outdoor lighting along the path from the driveway to the front door; motion detection lighting in low-traffic areas; adjustments to the font size on my mom's computer screen; keyless door locks, timing controlled lights in the house; "talking" microwave oven; pill organizers; self-adhesive bumps to be applied to dials and buttons on appliances to mark settings.

In my work with TransitionsUSA, I was face-to-face with the issues of daily living for those who had become physically or intellectually impaired and so I was vicariously witnessing many of the issues I imagined my own mother was experiencing. Because of my work, I began to anticipate problems and made efforts to correct them before they became an issue in my mother's home 2,800 miles away.

But today, taking my mom to the movie *Raising Helen* is my first experience with the insidious nature of "presumption": we—my brothers, their wives, Mom's husband, her oncologist and all the other medical specialists treating her—had assumed that my mother's vision loss was directly related to her disease and the radiation required to treat it.

Who knew that a trip to LensCrafters the next day would put my mother back in the driver's seat—quite literally, since she was able then to take her driver's license exam and pass, allowing her to resume many of the activities and freedoms she'd been living years without because of limited vision.

It was a life-changing moment for me: more than ever before, I resolved to think out of the box and stay open to every possibility in resolving issues that kept my mother from experiencing the fullest life possible, for as long as possible.

On a far deeper level than ever before, I took on the role of riding shotgun for Nancy, determined to mitigate any obstacles that interfered with a long and extended life for her and confident in my ability and determination to do so.

Mother and daughter: together, we would tackle anything.

It is 1985 and my mother and I are traveling from New York to Vermont, as we have done regularly over the years, to lay flowers on the gravesite of her high school sweetheart, my father, Frederick "Fritz" Muer. We plan to spend several days visiting Nancy's mother, my grandmother, and introducing her to her grandson Vincent. He's seven months old and this is his big trip to anywhere other than the neighborhood park.

If forced to choose between taking her next breath and traveling to anywhere she hadn't been before, my mother would grab a suitcase. In the ten years since Tom retired from the military, the two of them have been taking the Southern California countryside by storm in their twin Yamaha motorcycles. "Powered up" from the two bikes they owned while Tom was stationed in Japan, cycling has become their preferred method of travel and primary means of leisure and adventure. A recent two-week excursion through Bryce Canyon is now the benchmark against which all other trips are measured, and they have their eye on a cabin in the Southern California mountains less than a two hour scenic ride by bike from their home. Mom has been telling me all about their latest road trip and their ideas for a second home retreat as she travels somewhat uncomfortably in the confines of a traditional automobile.

"This is nice," Nancy says, gazing out the window from the passenger side. "No matter how many times we make this trip, I always enjoy it. There's nothing like visiting other parts of the country."

Then, as if suddenly inspired, she strains against her seat belt to reach back and adjust the blankets wrapped around baby Vince, clueless as he dozes in his car seat.

"Lucky for you being married to a career Marine officer," I observe. "'Join the Army, see the world.'"

"Seattle and Guam with your father," my mother agrees. "North Carolina, Hawaii, Texas, Virginia, Japan with Tom— and all the places we were able to visit from there. Not to mention the places in California."

"No moss growing under your feet!" I laugh affectionately, knowing nothing has changed. On any given day, Mom would rather be anyplace new than in her own home. "Where did you like living the best?"

"They each had their pluses and minuses," Mom answers to no surprise on my part. Ever the diplomat, this is a woman who, in the spirit of fairness and impartiality, has purchased a $50 birthday present every single year for each and every one of her adult children—never a dollar more or less. The big "tell" was one year when Jim threw out a gift idea that cost $77 and just like that, upped the ante for all of us!

"I often wonder how you managed all those years when Tom was deployed to Japan and Viet Nam and you had to raise four children on your own. Sam was only two the first time he left."

"You do what you have to do," my mom answers, nonchalantly dismissing the almost six years her husband was mostly away, leaving her to manage a family alone and on the limited income of a military family. "Besides, I had you and that was a big help."

"Yeah, those fun and frolicking childhood years I missed out on," I muse.

"I remember when you complained to your Aunt Marion that you skipped being a kid and jumped right into being a mom."

"I wasn't complaining," I object. "I didn't know anything different; I was just stating a fact."

"Do you have regrets about that?" my mom asks, looking up from touching Vince's nose, pulling on his ears, taking advantage of his inherent good humor when he's conked out.

"You do what you have to do," I answer affectionately and know my mother understands that I wouldn't change a thing.

"I'm just so tired," my grandmother says two days later as we say our goodbyes. Grandma has lived in her own apartment for the past thirty years, since my grandfather's death. But she has just moved to a skilled nursing facility, primarily because of confusion and forgetfulness, and our visit coincides with taking care of some of the details of the move. But mostly, we've just sat and visited and enjoyed four generations of companionship.

"Yeah, he can wear you out," I admit, nodding to Vince, who is comatose after almost non-stop attention as the featured act of our traveling show at the nursing home.

"No, It's not that," my grandmother says, beginning her goodbye hugs. "I wouldn't have missed your visit for the world. I'm just tired," she repeats.

"We'll see you soon," I say, kissing her cheek, and knowing I'll be making more frequent visits now that Vince is born.

But the next morning, only a few minutes before we are ready to walk out the door of my grandmother's now empty apartment to drive eight hours to New York to put Mom on her flight back to San Diego, the phone rings. It's my Uncle Bob.

"Priscilla's gone," he says somberly.

Priscilla Mae Hill, my grandmother, has passed quietly in the night.

Nancy, my mother, is 60.

Ten months earlier, before Vincent's birth and Priscilla's death, a nurse takes my vitals and says with measured patience, "I'm supposed to ask if you checked the meatloaf or the chicken for tonight."

"Did Mom say what she's having?" I ask.

"I think she wants to have what you're having. Or maybe she wants to have what you're not having so she can send up part of hers and you both can share two entrees. The message seems to have gotten garbled, if you can imagine that.

"But just between you and me," the nurse adds, "the chicken tastes like cardboard."

"What about the meatloaf?" I ask.

"Similar to dog food, but definitely better than cardboard," she answers, pulling my gown slightly open to gently examine the severe chest bruises left by the seatbelt of my car. Mom and I were coming from the mall after doing some baby shopping when another car collided with us head-on. Mom has a broken sternum and is in cardiac ICU on the 4th Floor; I am in ICU on the 6th Floor, attached to a fetal monitor. All things considered, the car being totaled and me being seven and a half months pregnant, we're doing great—except for logistically.

"Okay," I say, making an executive decision. "Tell her meatloaf and make sure she asks for lots of catsup."

"Good call," the nurse agrees, giving me a thumbs up. "I'll pass it along." She heads off to the nurse's station where someone there will call down to the nurse's station on 4th to convey the message to my mom, a system we've negotiated with the extreme indulgence of three shifts of nursing professionals. When Tom or Vinnie, my husband, are here, they do the running, but otherwise we rely on the kindness of strangers.

Moments later, a different ambassador pops his head in. It's Ralph from the first floor gift shop, somehow also inexplicably drawn into our messaging system. "Your mom says she may be transferred out of ICU tomorrow morning and into a room with a phone. She wants your telephone number on a piece of paper so she can call you right away."

I write it down and have no sooner sent it with him than a candy striper, Beth, stops in. "In answer to your question," she recites, "Nancy says she still prefers *Days of Our Lives* to *The Edge of Night*, but she'll watch whatever you do, just let her know."

"*Days of Our Lives* it is," I announce easily, since I don't care, and Beth dashes past Dr. Bertram, my obstetrician, who's just entering the room.

"Busy?" he asks congenially, looking after Beth.

"Not so much," I answer casually. "Maybe a little bored. It sure would be nice if my mom was up here with me."

"Yes, I hear you two are running the show around here," he smiles. "Staff productivity is down thirty-three percent," he jokes.

"Really?" I ask, half believing in the probability.

"Not so much," he laughs. "You know the hospital has a policy that prohibits two members of the same family from sharing a room."

I shrug and then wince, reminding myself not to do that again.

"No exceptions," he adds.

I give a wave of my hand as if it didn't matter one way or the other, although I've been protesting the policy non-stop since I arrived. I mean, after all, it's not like we aren't making the best of a bad situation. Either we are finding a whole lot more to say to each other since we've been hospitalized and bored, or the act of having to engage the physical assistance of those around us provides a greater visual demonstration of the fact that mother and daughter talk a lot.

My mind wanders to the baby shower scheduled next week and I make a mental note to have someone ask my mom if she wants roses or an orchid for her corsage. I already know the answer.

"But in this case," Dr. Bertram continues, "I've asked the hospital to make an exception."

This grabs my attention. "Come again?" I ask incredulously.

"We'll be moving you and your mother into the same room here on 6th tomorrow at noon."

"Seriously?"

"It's the least we can do for you," Dr. Bertram responds with exaggerated gravity, "not to mention the other patients in the hospital. I don't know what you've been doing to engage my staff so diligently, but hopefully, with the two of you in the same room, we can all get back to work."

"That's terrific!" I exclaim. "I feel better already."

"It's what we live for," the doctor answers and starts to leave.

"Dr. Bertram?"

"Yes?"

"When you have a chance, can you send in one of the nurses so I can relay the good news to my mother?"

It's the first time my mother has attended her high school reunion—in person. On all previous occasions, she's been there in spirit, using Ma Bell to linger on the phone and catch up on all the gossip with her core group of friends—a dozen classmates who, rather than paying the $8.25 to attend the Saturday night banquet, get together at Austin's house for a potluck and beer and include Mom via speaker phone.

But this is Mom's 65th Reunion; it's 2007 and Mom has spent the evening with friends who knew her when she was a child, a teen and later as the wife of their high school ski champion. I can see she is tired; I can also see she doesn't want the evening to end. I have savored the stories of the father I did not know; anecdotes from the days when Mom worked as a legal secretary at Hingham shipyard; tales of the children of her classmates and their children. I am feeling recharged by this connection to family and friends and can tell Mother is, too. We needed this.

We are staying with my cousin Rick and the next day, he rounds up my Uncle Red and the four of us hit the road to drop in on my cousin Jan, who lives in a neighboring town only six miles away.

How does one describe conversation among family members? We chit-chat about this and that, everything and nothing, cover again half the things talked about the night before but that Jan missed. We're into our second round of coffee and once again I am lulled into this restorative sense of companionship. But there is something different between this group than there was the night before, a unique thread of connection with these adults that I can't quite identify.

I think about it as the others talk, expressing their concern over how the dry spell is taking its toll on the local water supplies and how the dairy farmers are fretting the domino effect on their herds. I'm listening, but not listening as I try to put my finger on it...and then do: We are five grown adults, all of whom are bonded by the common experience of having endured unforeseen deaths in our lives.

Uncle Red shares the loss of his brother, my father and Mom's husband when he was still just a teen. But too, he has lost his wife, after standing by her side through eight years in a nursing home for treatment of Alzheimer's disease.

My cousin Rick is newly widowed, losing his wife to breast cancer. It was two years of a dismal, downhill struggle that has left him unpredictably alone at 68.

Cousin Jan, whose home we are gathered tonight, lost her husband five years ago to an unexpected, massive heart attack, leaving her widowed at a much younger age than she ever imagined.

Mom lost a husband while she was essentially still just a girl. Later, she lost her youngest son to what she always claimed was a broken heart, my brother suffering from a failed marriage and the alcohol and drug abuse he used to try to ease his pain. And then, her husband Tom died—in his seventies, but long before she was ready for life without him.

And my life has been a steady series of losses, beginning at birth with the father I would never know. Later, my brother would die; then my husband Vincent, father of my son. And four years earlier, over six crippling months, five people unexpectedly left this world, and me: my husband Vinnie's parents, my son's grandparents; Colin, my son's closest friend and the brother he never had; my husband after Vinnie, "Big John", after only ten years together; and Tom, the man who was my father when my birth father couldn't be there himself.

In this small group of us sharing coffee, I can feel our experience of death, grieving, and loss as an unspoken bond between us, invisible threads connecting our hearts in a way that most cannot see. The revelation comes as something of a surprise, but it feels reassuring in some kind of profound, inexplicable way.

As if reading my thoughts, my mother reaches over and gives my hand a squeeze and her smile warms me.

The words are felt but unspoken, "You do what you have to do."

"I've got an offer on my business, but it may take another few weeks to work out the details," I assure my mom with characteristic optimism. "Then I can be here every day, if necessary, to help you build up your strength."

The non-Hodgkin's lymphoma recurred two years ago. Mom immediately started treatments again, repeating them as often as her strength allowed, about every six months. This most recent therapy, however, has resulted in hospitalization. Mom is as pale as I've ever seen her, frail and exhausted. She lets me talk.

"I should be able to negotiate most of it from here in California, so I'll be at the house when you're released. There are things we can do to get it ready for you until you're able to be back on your feet. I've already talked to Tom and Jim about getting you to rehab and Vincent and I will do some rearranging of the furniture so you have everything you need at arm's reach, even though someone will always be there."

I am sitting at my mother's bedside, a cell phone ready in one hand and a pen and paper in the other, making a list as I talk.

"We can rent a lift for the bed or anything else you may need on the short-term until you have your strength back. We've started a visitation schedule so someone in the family will be here at the hospital with you at all times."

I jot down the words "bed lift", as if I would forget and punch "Google search" on my phone to find a local resource.

"Fritzi" . . . my mother's voice is far stronger than her physical body and the implied command of it stops me short and I raise my eyes to her. She holds my attention with a steady, almost pleading gaze and then says quite deliberately, "I'm tired. I'm really just so tired."

The echo of my grandmother's same words from years earlier startle me and fill me with dread.

"Fritzi," my mother repeats my name again. *"Do I have to do this anymore?"*

I don't recall a specific conversation in which my mother discussed the terms of how she would like to leave this world. But somehow, over the hundreds of thousands of hours we spent living under the same roof, talking by phone, emailing or traveling together, I inherently knew that she and I would be hand-in-hand when the critical moment in time arrived and that she trusted me with her last wishes.

I laid down my distractions, took both her hands in mine and collected myself before I answered. "Mom, you know I want to say yes, but I am here if your answer is no."

It was the most difficult thing I've ever had to say and I had to choke out the words. But I recognized instantly that Mom needed reassurance that even when her plan was different than mine, I would still be there for her—just as she had been for me. I didn't want to give up or give in, but I knew she alone would make the decision about how and when her life ended, and that my role, as daughter and best friend, would be to act on her behalf.

So when the nurse brought in her heart medication shortly thereafter, my mother refused to take it. I sat with her all night, notified Tom, Jim and Vince of her decision while she slept, and the following morning, with the entire family gathered at her side, Nancy Lee Turner closed her eyes and quietly passed.

As it had been for her when her own mother died, it was my 60th birthday.

It was during my marriage to John that I became casually interested in astrology. It started as a bit of fun to see who was what and whether the sign was a befitting description of those I knew or cared about. Some did, some didn't.

But Sagittarius applied to my mom as sure as the sun rises each morning. It amazed me time and again over the years just how true to the sign she was and gave me more than a little insight and delight!

Nancy was a light to those around her, inspirational in words and actions; she never lost hope, never failed to encourage a sense of optimism and anticipation about the future, believed in the "sunny side of life". She was honest to a fault and had no trouble telling me when she thought I was making a mistake or if a dress made my hips look wide. Throughout her life, she was in persistent pursuit of knowledge: she read the newspaper every day, was a regular at the library, enjoyed watching the history channel and others like it—national geographic, travel and biography. Whenever she could, she engaged others in conversation, learning from them about other countries, customs and beliefs.

More than anything, she loved to travel, loved being outdoors, thrived on the sense of adventure in visiting new places—countries, states, cities, attractions, restaurants. Change was an essential element in her thirst for life.

Mom met every obstacle to her health with tenacious optimism. But when Tom died, she lost her traveling companion. The limitations that placed on her being able to be out in the world were far more difficult for her to manage than any physical impairment she had endured.

It defied all her Sagittarius nature when, after the Non-Hodgkin's lymphoma returned, perhaps the best she could anticipate was a restricted subsistence within the four walls of her home, and I think she was simply unwilling to fight for a life she wouldn't, couldn't thrive in.

As for me, I was in the habit of finding solutions; like my mother, I lived by, "Do what you have to do". Whatever happened, I didn't worry about it, agonize over it, or try to figure it out. I just put the next foot in front of the other and did what was necessary to solve, resolve or minimize it.

In that pivotal moment in the hospital, the last night before my mother died, we were at odds. She didn't want the life she knew was left to her, and I didn't know any other way than to fight for her—and I thought, with her.

But with just a few simple words, my mother expressed all she wanted me to understand in that moment: She didn't want to fight; she wanted to let go. She was ready to move on, perhaps to what she may have viewed as her next great exploration, the unknown of life after death.

"Do I have to do this anymore?" is a reminder that in the end, we each have singular control over our own lives. And while it may seem impossibly difficult for those of us left behind, we could find that the kindest, most loving thing we can do for those we love, in the end, is let go.

All the art of living lies in a fine mingling
of letting go and holding on.
—Henry Havelock Ellis

Epilogue

*"Have you stopped to consider that
you helped them because you couldn't
be here to help your own mom?"*

My son Vince and I try to have dinner together once a week. It's nothing formal, no standing day or time, but despite both of us traveling for our work and keeping sometimes crazy schedules between work and personal lives, we are surprisingly successfully at making it happen.

Having "company" affords me an opportunity to prepare a meal using ingredients and the stovetop, foregoing my customary microwave or snack approach to evening dining, and I anticipate both this and his company.

I'm not an elaborate chef even on a good day, but I've improvised a tomato and basil sauce, leaning heavily on culinary tricks passed along by Vincent's paternal grandmother. It wasn't an easy path at first, but as she came to trust and embrace me as part of the family, she indoctrinated me into all things Italian.

I throw in a fresh salad consisting mostly of my neighbor's homegrown tomatoes, and pass off a loaf of homemade bread from the local farmer's market as if I'd spent the afternoon kneading dough myself. The result is a meal worthy of second helpings, which I refuse. But Vince, with his late twenties metabolism and thirty-four inch beltline, dives in with gusto.

"This is great, Mom," he says loading up his plate with a pile of pasta that exceeds my own carb allowance times ten. "Did you use Ragu or Prego?"

We share a relaxed laugh, comfortable with the wit and humor that has bolstered us through years of the unexpected twists and turns of life.

Typically, while we eat, we keep the conversation light, chit-chat really. Lots of observations and anecdotes about Abbey, the Sheperd-Chow mix we share raising, me during the week, he on weekends. Today we commiserate affectionately over her messy habit of toiling over a chew bone until it's a soft wad of mush and then abandoning it for the next newer, crunchier treat. The trail of soggy blobs dotted indiscriminately throughout the house have become testimony to our unwavering optimism that one day she'll actually finish one like other dogs do—parents ever hopeful that their child will "come around".

But once the dishes are cleared, we retreat to the family room with Chai Tea in hand, ready to settle into more consequential conversation. Vince stretches out on the long, leather couch, cozying up with Abbey, who stretches out alongside him, her head resting just at arm's reach so he can stroke her head or she can gnaw at his fingers, depending on her mood. I settle into the well-worn armchair at right angles to the couch, the same chair my mother always preferred over the thirty-four years she lived in this same house.

Then we let the conversation flow to our lives, our work, our relationships, our concerns. We talk meaningfully, not by design, but because we are friends as well as mother and son, and we rely on this time to think out loud or get a second opinion or to just feel understood.

Vince is tall and slender, with gentle eyes and a kind demeanor. I like watching him, admiring the adult he has become, the boy images of his journey to manhood morphed into a hologram of the man I see before me. I like how his mind works, his intelligence and his insight. He often surprises me with just how deeply he perceives and interprets the world around him, and today is one of those times.

I have been regularly updating him on the process of writing this book, a new experience for me and one which has prompted more self-examination than I could have anticipated. It has been a particularly imposing week, one in which I've worked on Chapter Ten culminating in my mother's death. It's been nearly two years now and a lot has happened over the months: I've finally made the move from New York, my home for over forty years, and into my mother's now vacant house in Vista, California, just north of San Diego. Too late to be with my mother, but now I am closer to my son and two brothers. It is what I have wanted to do since the death of my husband John in 2003, looking forward to finally being physically present on a daily basis with my mother, to ease her challenges of aging and be there as her best friend. Her death altered the original intention, but didn't change the momentum.

I am telling Vince about the challenge of putting into words some of what I experienced with her life and death, how examining the course of our relationship has given a name and face to feelings I had not yet fully faced—perhaps most difficult, those feelings of guilt and regret that I hadn't made it to California sooner rather than later.

"But I was here," Vince offers as matter-of-fact reassurance and consolation.

In 2005, my son moved from New York to the greater San Diego area for some much needed geographic relief from the memories and associations related to the six people we loved and lost in 2003. Though not by intention, once here and living not far from my mother, Vince became the eyes and ears that abated my long-distant concerns.

"Don't make it obvious," I would say, "but just stop by and see how she's doing."

"Mom," my son would respond patiently, "I'm there every Tuesday to take Gramma Nan's garbage down the drive. It's Wednesday, I would know if there was a problem."

"Okay, right," I would agree quickly. "So how's your Thursday looking?"

And we would laugh, me having every assurance that short of being there myself, no one was a better surrogate in words and deeds; and he knowing that whatever I may have asked of him, he would probably have already thought of himself as an expression of his own love and concern for his grandmother.

I think of the invaluable role he played for nearly five years, a crucial cog in the collective family machinery—my brothers, wives and children—that kept my mother safe and in her own home until the day she died. "We both know I would have made myself crazy with worry if you hadn't moved to California. Can I gush all over you with gratitude or did you get sick of hearing it after like the thousandth time?"

He waves his hand, brushing away the compliment as he always does.

"I still owe you," I elaborate unnecessarily.

"Big time," he agrees. "How 'bout taking Abbey for me next weekend? Football at Craig's house and canines aren't on the short list."

"I'll probably need a new bag of chew bones to carry us over."

"I'll double that if I can drop her off before noon."

"Deal."

"Have you stopped to consider that you helped them because you couldn't be here to help your own mom?"

Abbey's tail wags but her eyes remain closed, lost in restful repose in the warmth and physical comfort of Vince's leg.

"It's just that I keep thinking I should have been here myself," I persist. "Should have done more. . . ."

"Let's see," Vince ponders, stroking his chin for effect. "You talked to her at least once a day, exchanged emails every morning, sent your only child across the continent to act as a secret agent, personally flew from one coast to the other at least three times a year, initiated improvements to the house to minimize her vision loss and make her feel more secure and safe at home. . . ."

"Enough already," I complain. "You sound like an infomercial."

". . . .while simultaneously running your own business, helping thousands of people just like your mom move from homes they loved with at least a little, and in most cases, a lot less trauma and emotional agony. Yeah, I can see how you could really beat yourself up for not doing enough."

"When did you start talking like a promotional brochure?"

"You remember what you told me about why you started TransitionsUSA in the first place, Mom? Because you liked old people?"

I smile. "Well, 'like' is a bit of misnomer. More like I just seem to have a natural affinity for the concerns of people as they grow older."

"You say tomato, I say tomato," Vince shrugs and Abbey stirs just enough to cozy up a little closer. "And it never occurred to you that 'natural affinity' might be directly related to the concerns you had for your own mother?"

Actually, it hadn't. Even now as he points it out, it seems merely coincidental. It is my turn to shrug.

"What I'm suggesting," he says pushing up to a half-sitting position to make his point, causing Abbey's eyes to pop open and ears perk up, "is that if you'd been able to move to California sooner rather than later, there would have been this long trail of thousands of people whose lives were more difficult because you weren't there, not just the people you moved but their children and their families."

Vince is sitting up now and Abbey mistakes his ardor as a signal he's ready to play, strains to lick his face in excitement.

"How many times did you call Uncle Tom or Uncle Jim as you were leaving a client who had to move because of an accident in their own home, passing along ideas you got about things they could do to make Gramma Nan's home safer for her?"

This part was certainly true. I never orchestrated a move that I didn't examine the underlying "why"—why was it necessary for this person to move from their home?—with the pragmatic part of me searching for alternatives that might have kept them in their own familiar surroundings. It was my job to move them, but another part of me was keenly attentive to what might have kept them from having to move.

And of course, I was always eager to pass along these insights to my mother and brothers and son, hoping to avert disasters and avoidable mishaps that might have driven my mom from her own home.

"Call it 'guilt in action' if you want," Vince continues, kindly but firmly pushing Abbey away and out of his line of vision, "but it seems to me you couldn't be here for her, so you took your empathy and 'can-do' conviction to those you could help. *Have you stopped to consider that you helped them because you couldn't be here to help your own mom?*"

It wasn't until this conversation with my son that I really recognized that over all the years of relocating adult seniors from their homes to community living, a part of me was always seeing my mother in them and projecting how I knew she would feel if we children found it necessary to move her out of the house and home she had resided in for nearly thirty-five years. And as unsettling and painful as I knew it would be for her, I could also feel how excruciating it would be for us, her children.

Even at that time, I really couldn't imagine a more devastating blow to my mother's life or her well-being or her children's peace-of-mind.

Through TransitionsUSA, I dedicated myself to helping make moving transitions as bearable as possible. Through my son's insight, I finally understood how serving others in that way helped appease my geographic inability to facilitate my mother's own well-being in her home.

I paid attention to the "why" of the move, and of course, almost always at the root of the action was love and concern: children who wanted to assure that their parents, mother or father, were safer, more comfortable, more accessible to family and grandchildren and those who loved them. At the same time, the part of me that was always looking after my own mother also took measure of those things that might have kept them in their homes.

I must have moved hundreds of people whose lives took a sudden turn from a fall in their homes, though I used the example of Steve and Barbara in Chapter Six because their son's reactive and proactive response was so immediate that it left both parents bewildered and second-guessing. But consider these most recent statistics:

- One in three adults aged 65 and older falls each year. Of those who fall, 20% to 30% suffer moderate to severe injuries that make it hard for them to get around or live independently, and increase their risk of early death.

- Older adults are hospitalized for fall-related injuries five times more often than they are for injuries from other causes.

- In 2011, emergency departments treated 2.4 million nonfatal fall injuries among older adults; more than 689,000 of these patients had to be hospitalized.*

- Twenty to thirty percent of people who fall suffer moderate to severe injuries such as lacerations, hip fractures, or head traumas. These injuries can make it hard to get around or live independently, and increase the risk of early death.

- Falls are the most common cause of traumatic brain injuries (TBI). TBI's are a major cause of death and disability in the United States, contributing to about 30% of all injury deaths.

I am scientifically and gadget inclined, and not long after meeting and moving Steve and Barbara, I discovered a delightful little 3" x 4", battery operated, LED device called Mr. Beams that lights up for 60 seconds when it detects motion. If it had been positioned on the floor next to the bed, it would have detected Steve's feet hitting the floor and illuminated the area long enough for him to find (or notice) his slippers and make his way to the bathroom just as he'd done uneventfully for as long as he'd lived!

(Mr. Beams' usefulness is limited only by my own creativity. I have one in my bathroom, which is a far less glaring light in the night than a 60-watt bulb. There's one in the hallway which lights up when Abbey is trying to get my attention to be let out for her own bathroom break during the night. The practical reality is that Mr. Beams and I are

*Center for Disease Control, "Costs of Falls Among Older Adults"

best friends: he lights up my car trunk, my coat closet and the kitchen pantry.)

An under-the-bed, rollaway shoe drawer might require a little getting used to, but is also effective in keeping the floor clear of obstacles that cause falls.

The practical reality is that there are half a dozen problem-solving alternatives for safely getting up in the night for those who have reached an age when falling can mean the difference between living independently and being forced into a compromised, lifestyle change.

After my mother passed, I decided to capitalize on the perspective I'd gained from TransitionsUSA and my own personal experiences, and shifted from providing services to facilitate leaving the home, to instead helping adults stay in their homes. I created a company called Household Guardians, and dedicated myself to helping my clients create better homes for safer living. Today, I offer ideas, alternatives and modifications to improve houses and living at home so that adults can reduce falls, accidents, and the discomforts that come with aging.

I am supported by the limitless possibilities of today's technology, which quite literally offers solutions to just about every possible issue we may experience as age takes its toll on our eyesight, hearing and general physical prowess. There is much we can do to avoid falls (short of regaining our youthful bounce and balance!) and there is equally as much we can do to minimize the severity of a fall if it happens.

Of course, living comfortably and safely in our homes is far more than just preventing falls—the scope of what it encompasses can't be listed, but essentially it's about helping adults move through their daily routines with less intrusion on their lifestyle, with less inconvenience. We want to continue to prepare meals, but can take advantage of devices that make up for arthritic or unsteady hands, knives that greatly reduce the risk of slips and cuts, cookware that is light and "burn-free", timers that are readable and easy to use—whatever the concern, there's a solution!

If you have trouble touching your toes or bending at the waist, there are literally dozens of products on the market now that will help you put on your socks, lift your legs into bed or pick up something from the floor.

Simple modifications to a computer can make it easier to read the screen or even let it read to you; keyboards are available with vastly larger letters and easier facility for typing. Lights can be controlled from a single remote or made to operate automatically on a timer; managing lighting has innumerable dimensions that cover every area of the interior and exterior of a house. "Grab bars" are now stylishly being referred to as balance bars and are marketed by high end manufacturers for luxury and, incidentally, safety. The choices available for aging adult bathroom convenience and comfort can leave you breathless—but in a good way!

I've discovered that my perspective is keener and more insightful than most because of my years with TransitionsUSA and the ongoing focus and intention I had around caring for my mother. I recently viewed the home of eighty-something parents, where the son had spent significant time and money to make their home safer for them to live. In less than an hour, I found 22 additional, inexpensive changes he could implement that would significantly improve everyone's confidence in their well-being.

Household Guardians is also about educating and improving communication between the two generations. Over the years I've added to it, but after my experience with Patty in Chapter Seven where the symptoms of her mother's mental decline went unnoticed, I started a check-list that adult children can utilize to help identify warning signals and areas where their parents may need guidance, assistance, or intervention. There are any number of online sites and apps that provide fun and entertaining exercises that evaluate various aspects of alertness and memory and can be performed daily to increase and maintain brain function.

The concept of helping aging adults stay in their homes has gained momentum in recent years, and has become popularly coined as "Aging in Place". The National Association of Home Builders (NAHB) offers training and certification as a specialist in this growing segment, which has attracted many in the remodeling industry, particularly interior designers. Household Guardians offers that expertise also and can make recommendations that include significant remodeling improvements such as repositioning electrical outlets, lowering cabinet heights, changing cabinet knobs and pulls, and installing appliances that are specifically geared toward the ease and comfort of those over 65.

But because of my experience as a National Center for Healthy Homes Hazard Ratings Specialist, Household Guardians goes one step further for those considering major remodeling by providing an in-depth assessment for issues in the overall environment that might be interfering with a resident's general health and well-being (the presence of mold, lead paint, chemicals, pesticides; the addition of railings, lighted walkways; a study of how people cope in their own space).

According to the AARP, by 2015, those aged 50 and older will represent 45% of the population. This same group controls over 75% of the country's wealth. Many of these Baby Boomers will have participated in decisions that resulted in moving their parents from their homes and are imprinted with the trauma endured by both sides of the experience. Studies show these Boomers are motivated not to have to endure the same uprooting and have the money to invest in technology, changes and modifications to their home that will keep them living there safely, comfortable, and ably for as long as possible—and hopefully, far longer than their own parents. I believe all the years of my professional and personal experiences have led me to help them do this—for Baby Boomers looking into their near future, and for Baby Boomers who are still watching over their seventy-or eighty plus parents.

Two, five or ten years from now, I hope to be sharing a far different collection of stories—those of aging adults and their adult children who found ways to extend their lifetimes in their own homes to live with greater ease, comfort, productivity, independence and yes . . .

Grace AND *Grit.*

*Destiny is a name often given in retrospect
to choices that had dramatic consequences.*

—J.K. Rowling

Resources

American Society on Aging
www.asaging.org
The American Society on Aging is an association of diverse individuals bound by a common goal: to support the commitment and enhance the knowledge and skills of those who seek to improve the quality of life of older adults and their families. The membership of ASA is multidisciplinary and inclusive of professionals who are concerned with the physical, emotional, social, economic and spiritual aspects of aging.

American Association of Retired Persons (AARP)
www.aarp.org
AARP is a nonprofit, nonpartisan organization that helps people 50 and older improve the quality of their lives.

National Council on Aging
www.ncoa.org
The National Council on Aging (NCOA) is the nation's leading nonprofit service and advocacy organization representing older adults and the community organizations that serve them. For more than 60 years, NCOA has been a trusted voice and innovative problem-solver helping seniors navigate the challenges of aging in America. They work with local and national partners to give older adults tools and information to stay healthy and secure, and they advocate for programs and policies to improve the lives of all seniors, especially the most vulnerable.

Area Councils on Aging

www.n4a.org

Local agencies that provide a range of services for older adults that are part of the NCOA network throughout the United States.

Alzheimers Association

www.alz.org

Formed in 1980, the Alzheimer's Association advances research to end Alzheimer's and dementia while enhancing care for those living with the disease. There are local chapters throughout the U.S. Locations can be found at this website.

Braille Institute

www.brailleinstitute.org

Braille Institute is a nonprofit organization whose mission is to eliminate barriers to a fulfilling life caused by blindness and severe sight loss.

They offer a variety of free programs, classes and services at five centers and 220 community outreach locations throughout Southern California.

Each year Braille Institute serves more than 75,000 people. They provide an environment of hope and encouragement through integrated educational, social, and recreational programs and through our services, classes, and seminars.

Macular Degeneration Foundation

www.eyesight.org

The Macular Degeneration Foundation is dedicated to those who have and will develop macular degeneration. They offer this growing community the latest information, news, hope and encouragement. Services include links to resources such as Low Vision Centers, Therapists, Physicians, and Support

Groups in local areas. In addition, the Foundation gives financial support to researchers investigating treatments and others helping those coping with the challenges of living with the loss of their central vision.

National Association of Senior Move Managers
www.nasmm.org
Their mission is to facilitate the physical and emotional aspects of relocation for older adults, to increase industry awareness, to establish a national referral network, to enhance the professional competence of members, and to promote the delivery of services with compassion and integrity.

National Center for Healthy Housing
www.centerforhealthyhousing.org
The National Center for Healthy Housing (formerly the National Center for Lead-Safe Housing) was founded in 1992 to bring the housing, environmental, and public health communities together to combat childhood lead poisoning. Their mission is to develop and promote practical methods to protect children from environmental health hazards in their homes while preserving affordable housing.

Household Guardians
www.householdguardians.com
Household Guardians is a home safety and accessibility consulting firm whose mission is to facilitate the ability for families to make the smart, affordable changes to a home to ensure that older adults can remain safely and independent. The home safety assessments, makeovers and home safety product kits are part of the comprehensive offering package.

Several additional online sites and forums offer answers and solutions to the issues of aging, caregiving and making our best lives possible.

www.Agingcare.com

www. Caring.com

www. Eldercarematters.com

www. Seniorportal.com

Fritzi Gros-Daillon, CEO and founder of Household Guardians, is a highly successful entrepreneur in senior move management, environmental consulting, and most recently, the aging-in-place field. Her passion for keeping family members safe in their own home environment for as long as is reasonably possible has grown from watching families struggle with choices and decisions about the issues of staying home or downsizing. The goal is to maximize longevity and independence in the home environment of choice while minimizing the stress and worry.

She earned her Masters in Business Policy at Columbia University and combined with her environmental business background, certification as a Living by Design Specialist and years of experience, Fritzi brings a combination of expertise and perspective to the current aging-in-place issues. As a senior move manager, she worked with 1,000 families over ten years in New York. Currently based in Southern California, she provides consulting services that include planning and implementation of home safety solutions. Having spent many years as a long-distance caregiver for her parents, she shares her experience from a personal and professional viewpoint.

About the Speaker

Fritzi Gros-Daillon is passionate about her desire to help two generations—seniors and their adult children as they face the tough issues of aging-in-place and making downsizing decisions. She brings understanding to the issues, information about services, and desperately needed options to people who are just beginning this journey or who have already traveled along its path. She shares her expertise and very personal experience in working with several hundred families over the years. She has delivered the message at national conventions on healthy homes, senior moving management and aging in America. Fritzi also speaks locally and regionally to audiences in community centers, chambers of commerce, churches, schools and clubs.

A sample of topics include:

There's No Place Like MY Home

Topics on safety throughout the home environment with practical tips for implementation by family members and/or professional service providers.

Who Gets Grandma's Yellow Pie Plate?™

Family-focused workshop on the disposition of our personal possessions, the options and implications of the decisions for the individual and the family.

Decision Time for Families-Stay or Downsize?

Workshop for boomers with aging parents about the signs of change, communication skills and decisions that reflect each generation's desire for independence, respect and control.

Safety is Freedom

Workshop providing the steps to ensure that our home fits our current lifestyle and is adaptable for the future, giving us the freedom to pursue other interests without the nagging stress of the "what ifs".

For more details, a full list of topics and to schedule a talk, please contact:

Fritzi Gros-Daillon
Professional Home Safety & Aging-at-Home Consultant
MS, CLDS, CAC, CDPH I/A
NCHH Hazard Rating Specialist
www.HouseholdGuardians.com
fritzi@householdguardians.com

www.facebook.com/HouseholdGuardians
twitter.com/HHGuardians
www.pinterest.com/hhguardians/
www.linkedin.com/company/household-guardians